MAIMONIDES

MAIMONIDES
His Life and Works

by

DAVID YELLIN and ISRAEL ABRAHAMS

Third, Revised Edition

With Introduction, Bibliography and

Supplementary Notes

by

JACOB I. DIENSTAG

HERMON PRESS
NEW YORK

MAIMONIDES: His Life and Works
Revised Edition
New Matter © 1972
Hermon Press, New York
L.C.C. No. 72-83937
ISBN 0-87203-031-8

CONTENTS

Contents

CHAPTER VII

CHAPTER VIII

CHAPTER IX

CHAPTER X

CHAPTER XI

CHAPTER XII

Introduction to the Revised Edition

by

JACOB I. DIENSTAG

The publication of a new edition of this work
is a testimony to the quality of this biography
of Maimonides which first appeared close to
seventy years ago. Originally published simultaneously in England and the United States in
1903, it had readily attained semi-classical sta-
tus. It was reprinted in England, 1935, and the
United States, 1936, and had received the compliment of translation into Italian. (1)

In editing this new revised edition, (2) we
have been conscious of a wise remark uttered
by Professor Harry Austryn Wolfson: "For by
its mere publication, a book does not become to
its maker a closed masoretic text." We, therefore felt that we could greatly enhance the value
of this work by bringing up to date the notes
and bibliographical sources reflecting the scholarship on the subject during the last seventy
years. In the supplementary notes which follow
those of the authors near the end of the book,
we have attempted to provide material not
touched upon by the authors, and whenever
possible, to elaborate upon *their* notes. (3)

For the convenience of the readers we have

Introduction

included a selected bibliography of Maimonides' works in English translation and major works about him, shedding light upon his life and thought.

Since the last impression of this work in 1936, the co-author of this work, David Yellin, has passed away. We find it therefore appropriate to present brief sketches of both him and his deceased colleague, Israel Abrahams, who have made their imprint on Jewish scholarship.

DAVID YELLIN

David Yellin, the son of Joshua Yellin, one of the leaders of the Jerusalem community, was born in that city, March 19, 1864 and died there, December 12, 1941. As a Hebrew philologist and Orientalist, Yellin distinguished himself as a pioneer in the modern Hebrew educational system in Jerusalem in defiance of the ultra religious Jews' opposition to his modern innovations. A descendant of both Ashkenazic and Oriental Jews (his mother was a member of the Sassoon family of Baghdad), Yellin combined within himself the values he derived from both branches of Jewry. He received a traditional religious and general education in English, Arabic, Turkish, French and German. After following a career of teaching in various schools, he was appointed in 1926 as lecturer

Introduction

and in 1936 as professor of medieval Hebrew poetry at the Hebrew University.

Yellin's academic and scholarly interests did not interfere with his communal activities on behalf of the Jewish settlement in Palestine and the Zionist movement during the critical period when tension between the Jews and the Mandatory power was at its height. Yellin was for many years considered leader of the Jewish community. As founder and president of the first B'nai Brith lodge in Jerusalem, he made many trips throughout Egypt and Turkey and served as a representative of the Jews to the Turkish government, and actively supported the Young Turk movement of 1908. From 1920 to 1928, he was the head of the *Vaad Leumi,* the National Council of Jews in Palestine under the British Mandate. Yellin visited the United States three times in order to solicit support for the newly established schools and seminaries in Palestine. During his visit in 1924, he lectured at the Jewish Institute of Religion and Columbia University.

In a selected bibliography published in the *Jubilee Volume* in honor of his 70th birthday (Jerusalem, 1935), are enumerated 95 entries covering some of the literary activities of Yellin in the field of Hebrew philology, Biblical exegesis, medieval Hebrew literature and poet-

Introduction

ry, Palestine, pedagogy and education; also translations into Hebrew from Turkish, English and Arabic, too numerous to list here. We cannot, however, on this occasion, omit Yellin's contribution to Maimonidean scholarship:

a) *Rabenu Mosheh ben Maimon* (Warsaw, 1898). One of the first scholarly biographies of the Sage written in Hebrew which served as a basis for the present work before us.

b) *Two Autograph Leaves in the writing of Maimonides* (*Tarbiz*, vol. I, no. 3, 1939). Contains fragments from the Arabic original of Maimonides' *Guide for the Perplexed* in his own handwriting with explanatory notes by Yellin.

c) *Fragment of R. Meir Abulafia's Kitab al-Rasa'il* (*Kirjath Sepher*, vol. VI, 1930).
   Contains the correspondence between Maimonides and the Scholars of Lunel concerning the Maimonidean controversy. Yellin edited the Arabic original, accompanied by his Hebrew translation.

d) *A Characteristic of Maimonides* (*Ha-Aretz Maimonides Anniversary Volume*, 1935).

ISRAEL ABRAHAMS

Israel Abrahams, one of the most distinguished

Introduction

scholars produced by British Jewry, was born in
London, November 26, 1858 and died in Cambridge, October 6, 1925. He was educated at
London University and Jews' College where he
subsequently taught English, mathematics and
homiletics, from 1881 to 1902. He succeeded
Solomon Schechter as Reader in Rabbinic and
Talmudic literature at the University of Cambridge. Not confined to his own personal scholarship, Abrahams was instrumental in establishing various media for the advancement of
Jewish culture and scholarship. He was founder
and first president of the Jewish Historical
Society of England (1904) and editor of its
Transactions and joint editor, with Claude G.
Montefiore, of the *Jewish Quarterly Review*
from 1888 to 1908. Although not a Zionist, he
advocated the idea of a Hebrew University in
Jerusalem and was keenly interested in Palestine
as a cultural center.

Abrahams exercised a far-reaching influence
upon the cultural level of English speaking
Jewry by his unusual lucidness and felicity of
style. Very few scholars can claim with Abrahams such purity and beauty of style and at the
same time such richness and variety of learning.
As Reader in Rabbinics at Cambridge University, he became, by his sheer personality, the
interemediary between Jewish and Christian
scholarship, and helped to remove many deep-

seated prejudices prevalent in Christian circles.(4) He may have paved the way for many chairs in Jewish studies established in schools of higher learning in Great Britain and other English-speaking countries.

A prolific writer, the bibliography of his literary creativity published in the *Abrahams Memorial Volume* occupies about twenty-seven pages. A description of these works is beyond the scope of his survey. Some of his many articles were published in book form under the titles: *Chapters in Jewish Literature* (1899); *Book of Delight* (1912); *By-Paths in Hebraic Bookland* (1920). He was also a contributor to the *Encyclopedia Britannica, Encyclopedia of Religion and Ethics, Jewish Encyclopedia* and *Encyclopedia Biblica.* His *Companion to the Authorized Daily Prayer Book* (1914; 2nd ed. New York, Hermon Press, 1966) is a major contribution to scholarship on Jewish liturgy and is the first of its kind in English, His *Jewish Life in the Middle Ages* (1896; 2nd ed. 1932) exposed the English speaking world to the inner life of the Jewish people; its joys and sorrows, its communal and religious organization, social morality, home life, love and courtship. Abrahams edited and translated *Hebrew Ethical Wills* (1926). This work, which is accompanied by notes and introductions to each of the wills, also contains the will attributed to Maimonides.

Introduction

Abrahams' interest in Maimonides is also displayed in the review articles he wrote:

a) Critical notice of Friedlaender's *Guide of the Perplexed* (*Mind,* vol XI, 1886, p 97-106).

b) The Eight Chapters (*Jewish Chronicle,* Dec. 27, 1912, p 27-28). A review of Joseph Gorfinkle's edition of the *Eight Chapters of Maimonides on Ethics.*

———

The work before us is the result of a fortunate form of collaboration. Based upon Yellin's Hebrew edition of the *Life of Maimonides* (Warsaw, 1898), the biography is not a translation but is entirely rewritten to suit the non-Hebrew reader. While it is the result of both men's scholarship, the English version is, however, distinctly the work of Abrahams, whose notable grace of style we have referred to above. Their joint effort in producing this scholarly and yet readable biography of the Sage of Cordoba belies the famous saying of Rudyard Kipling, "East is East and West is West and never the twain shall meet." Yellin of Jerusalem and Abrahams of London produced for the English-speaking world a long needed biography of Maimonides which had not been available in

Introduction

English since Abraham Benisch's book appeared in 1847.

A final word should be said about the relationship of Abrahams and Yellin. Although they were worlds apart in their Jewish political outlook; Abrahams an opponent of political Zionism and Yellin an ardent Jewish nationalist and one of the architects of the Jewish State, there was a profound mutual respect and affection between the two gentle scholars. Yellin respected Abrahams' scholarship and translated into Hebrew the latter's *Jewish Life in the Middle Ages* (*Ha-Shiloah*, v. 4, 1898-1899), *The Jewish Chronicle* reported an interview Abrahams had with Yellin (Sept. 14, 1900, p. 15). "Visitors to Jerusalem," Abrahams declared, "have always carried away with them affectionate regard for Mr. Yellin. Hence his presence in London has been welcomed with enthusiasm..." Abrahams, during a visit to Jerusalem, had an opportunity of witnessing the successful results of Yellin's pedagogical principles which he incorporated in his Hebrew text book *Le-fi ha-taf*. He persuaded the Jewish Study Society in England to authorize an English translation of Yellin's work, and he collaborated with Alice Lucas in producing this version.(5)

---

1) Maimonide; traduzione autorizzata del dr. Leone Luzzatto. Roma: Casa editrice Israel, 5688-1928.

Introduction

2) The present reprint is based upon the London edition.

3) In order to distinguish between the authors' footnote numbers and those provided by the editor for the supplementary notes, an asterisk (*) was added to the number, e.g. 1*, 2*, 3*, etc.

4) F. J. Feakes Jackson, "Israel Abrahams at Cambridge," *Israel Abrahams Memorial Volume,* New York, 1927, p. xliii-lix.

5) Hebrew Lesson Book; being an introduction to Mr. David Yellin's method of teaching Hebrew. Prepared for English readers by Alice Lucas and Israel Abrahams. London, 1903.

A Selected Bibliography of Books by and about Maimonides in English

A. WORKS OF MAIMONIDES

I. *MISHNEH TORAH* (The Code of Maimonides).

BOOK OF MISHNAH TORAH; Yod Ha-Hazakah by...Moses son of Maimon...With RABD'S Criticism and references translated in English by...Simon Glazer, Volume I. New York: Maimonides Publishing Co., 1927.

Text in Hebrew and English of Book I: Book of Knowledge niparallel columns. Added title page in Hebrew.

THE MISHNEH TORAH by Maimonides.

Book I [Book of Knowledge]. Edited according to the Bodleian (Oxford) Codex with introduction, Biblical and Talmudical references, notes and English translation by Moses Hyamson. New York: Bloch Publishing Co., 1937.
(Reprinted: Jerusalem, Boys Town Publishers, 1962.)

Also Hebrew title page. This edition is a side by side reprint of the manuscript and paged accordingly: recto and verso of manuscript and translation of same cover 4 pages.

THE MISHNEH TORAH by Maimonides.

Book II [Book of Adoration]. Edited according to the Bodleian (Oxford) Codex with Biblical and Talmudical references and with an English translation by Moses Hyamson...The Talmudical references and Hebrew footnotes by Rabbi Chaim M. Brecher.

New York: Bloch Publishing Co., 1949.

Also Hebrew title page; paged as above. (Reprinted: Jerusalem, Boys Town Publishers, 1962).

MAIMONIDES' MISHNEH TORAH (Yad Hazakah).

Edited from rare manuscripts and early texts, vocalized, annotated and provided with introductions by Philip Birnbaum.

New York: Hebrew Publishing Co., (c. 1967). (English and Hebrew on opposite pages). Abridged. Added title page in Hebrew.

THE CODE OF MAIMONIDES.

Book III. Book of Seasons [Treatise 1-7, 9-10]. Translated from the Hebrew by Solomon Gandz and Hyman Klein. With an Appendix by Ernest Wiesenberg. 1961.

(Yale Judaica Series, vol. xiv).

Book III: [Book of Seasons]. Treatise 8: Sanctification of the New Moon.

Translated from the Hebrew by Solomon Gandz . . . with supplementation and an introduction by Julian Obermann . . . and an astro-

Selected Bibliography

nomical commentary by Otto Neugebauer. 1956. (Yale Judaica Series, vol. xi).

Book V: Book of Holiness. Translated from the Hebrew by Louis J. Rabinowitz and Philip Grossman. 1965. (Yale Judaica Series, vol. xvi).

Book VI: Book of Asseverations. Translated from the Hebrew by B. D. Klien. 1962. (Yale Judaica Series, vol. xv).

Book VIII: Book of Temple Service. Translated from the Hebrew by Mendell Lewittes. 1957) (Yale Judaica Series, vol. xii).

Book IX: Book of Offerings. Translated by Herbert Danby. 1950. (Yale Judaica Series, vol iv).

Book X: Book of Cleanness. Translated from the Hebrew by Herbert Danby. 1954. (Yale Judaica Series, vol viii).

Book XI: Book of Torts. Translated from the Hebrew by Hyman Klein. 1954. (Yale Judaica Series, vol ix).

Book XII: Book of Acquisition. Translated from the Hebrew by Isaac Klein. 1951. (Yale Judaica Series, vol. v).

Book XIII: Book of Civil Laws. Translated from the Hebrew by Jacob J. Rabinowitz. 1949. (Yale Judaica Series, vol. ii).

Book XIV: Book of Judges. Translated from the Hebrew by Abraham M. Hershman. 1949. (Yale Judaica Series, vol. iii).

New Haven: Yale University Press. The translation is in progress.

Selected Bibliography

II. *SEPHER HA-MIZWOT* (Book of Divine Commandments).

THE BOOK OF DIVINE COMMAND-MENTS (the *Sefer ha-Mitzvoth* of Moses Maimonides) translated from the Hebrew with foreword and explanatory notes by Rabbi Charles Chavel... Volume I: The Positive Commandments. London: Soncino Press, 1940. "This present English translation is based upon the standard Hebrew text of the *'Sefer Ha-Mitzvoth'* [composed by R. Moses Ibn Tibbon], corrected wherever necessary on the basis of comparisons with the version printed by [Rabbi Chaim] Heller." (p. xxiv).

Contents:

a) Summary of the Fourteen Roots which Maimonides placed at the head of this work.

b) The 613 Commandments (abridged) which precede the Mishnah Torah.

c) The Positive Commandments.

d) Substitute Commandments.

e) The Seven Rabbinic Positive Commandments.

f) The Plan of the Sanctuary.

g) The Thirteen Basic Principles of Faith.

h) Fundamental Principles of Reward and Punishments in Judaism.

i) Bibliography. j) Glossary. k) Abbreviations.

l) General Index.

Selected Bibliography

THE COMMANDMENTS. Sefer Ha-Mitz-voth of Maimonides... Translated from the Hebrew with foreword, notes, glossary, appendices and indices by Rabbi Dr. Charles B. Chavel... 2 vols. London: Soncino Press (c 1967).

This is a new English translation, which covers the Negative Commandments also, is based throughout on the new Hebrew translation by R. Joseph Kapach, published by *Mosad Harav Kook* (Jerusalem, 5718).

Contents: Besides the items enumerated in the 1940 edition of this work, the translator has also added the following:

a) Criticism of Maimonides' list of the Commandments.
b) Performance of the Mitzvoth.
e) The Negative Commandments.
d) Maimonides' Doctrine of the Truth underlying the Commandments.
e) Positive and Negative Commandments applicable today.
f) The Fourteen Principles on which Maimonides based Sefer Ha-Mitzvoth.

III. *COMMENTARY ON MISHNAH ABOTH & SHEMONAH PERAKIM.*

THE COMMENTARY TO MISHNAH ABOTH. Translated, with an introduction and notes, and a translation of Mishnah Aboth by Arthur David. New York: Bloch (c. 1968).

Selected Bibliography

THE EIGHT CHAPTERS OF MAIMON-
IDES ON ETHICS (*Shemonah Perakim*); a
psychological and ethical treatise. Edited, anno-
tated, and translated with an introduction by
Joseph I. Gorfinkle... New York: Columbia
University Press, 1912. (Reprinted: New York
AMS Press, 1966)

IV. *EPISTLE TO YEMEN.*

MOSES MAIMONIDES' EPISTLE TO
YEMEN... An English translation by Boaz
Cohen.

In: Moses Maimonides' Epistle to Yemen;
the Arabic original and the three Hebrew versions, edited from manuscripts with introduction and notes by Abraham S. Halkin... New
York: American Academy for Jewish Research,
1952.

V. *THE PHILOSOPHICAL WRITINGS OF MAIMONIDES*

THE GUIDE OF THE PERPLEXED OF
MAIMONIDES. Translated from the original
and annotated by M. Friedlander... New York:
Hebrew Publishing Co., [1946].

Three parts bound in one volume; anastatic
reprint of London, 1871-1885 edition accompanied by notes omitted in all other editions.

THE GUIDE FOR THE PERPLEXED BY
MOSES MAIMONIDES. Translated from the

Selected Bibliography

original Arabic text by M. Friedlander ... New York: Dover Publications, [1956].

Reprint of second edition (1904) in which "the three volumes of the first edition have been reduced to one volume by the elimination of the notes; Hebrew words and phrases have been eliminated or translated" (preface).

MAIMONIDES. THE GUIDE OF THE PERPLEXED. An abridged edition with introduction and commentary by Julius Guttmann. Translated from the Arabic by Chaim Rabin... London: East and West Library, 1952. (Philosophia Judaica).

THE GUIDE FOR THE PERPLEXED BY MOSES MAIMONIDES. Translated with an introduction and notes by Shlomo Pines with an introductory essay by Leo Strauss. Chicago: The University of Chicago Press, 1963.

MAIMONIDES' TREATISE ON LOGIC... The original Arabic and three Hebrew translations critically edited on the basis of manuscripts and early editions and translated into English by Israel Efros.

New York: American Academy for Jewish Research, 1938.

VI. *MEDICAL WORKS.*

THE MEDICAL WRITINGS OF MAI-

Selected Bibliography

MONIDES. Published under the auspices of Israel Torah Research Institute, Jerusalem.

Vol. I Treatise on Asthma. Edited by Suessman Muntner. Philadelphia and Montreal: J. B. Lippincott Co., (c. 1963).

With preface by Béla Schick; Introduction by M. Murray Peshkin; "Maimonides the Physician" by Morris Fishbein.

Vol. 2: Treatise on Poisons and their Antidotes. Edited by Suessman Muntner. Philadelphia and Montreal: J. B. Lippincott Co., (c. 1966).

Vol. 3: Treatise on Hemorrhoids; Medical Answers (Responsa). Translated and edited by Fred Rosner and Suessman Muntner. Philadelphia and Toronto: J. B. Lippincott Co. (c. 1969).

MAIMONIDES "ON SEXUAL INTERCOURSE" Fi l'Jima. Translated from the Arabic (!) [by Ismar Lipshutz] with an introduction and commentary. Edited by Morris Gorlin. Brooklyn: Rambash Publishing Co., [1961]. (Medical historical studies of medieval Jewish medical works. vol. I). English translation based on Kroner's German translation. Made use of E. Seidel's review of Kroner's edition in *Mitteilungen zur Geschichte der Medizin und Naturwissenschaften,* vol. 17 (1918), p. 49-54.

MOSES BEN MAIMON. THE PRESERVA-

Selected Bibliography

TION OF YOUTH; Essays on Health. Translated from the Original Arabic...and with an introduction by Hirsch L. Gordon. New York: Philosophical Library, (c. 1958).

MOSES MAIMONIDES' TWO TREATISES ON THE REGIMEN OF HEALTH...Translated from the Arabic and edited in accordance with the Hebrew and Latin versions by Ariel Bar Sela, Hebbel E. Hoff, and Elias Faris. *American Philosophical Society. Transactions,* vol. 54, part 4 (1964). Philadelphia: American Philosophical Society, July 1964.

THE MEDICAL APHORISMS OF MOSES MAIMONIDES. Volume I. Translated and edited by Fred Rosner and Suessman Muntner. New York, Yeshiva University, 1970. (Studies in Judaica).

THE MEDICAL APHORISMS OF MOSES MAIMONIDES. Volume II. Translated and edited by Fred Rosner and Suessman Muntner. New York, Yeshiva University, 1972. (Studies in Judaica).

B. ANTHOLOGIES AND SELECTIONS

COHEN, ABRAHAM
The Teachings of Maimonides. By the Rev. A. Cohen. London, 1927. (Reprinted with Prolegomenon by Marvin Fox: New York: Ktav, 1968.)

Selected Bibliography

GLATZER, NAHUM N.
Maimonides said. An anthology, selected and translated by Nahum N. Glatzer. New York: The Jewish Book Club, [c. 1941].

HILL, JEFF
The Wisdom of Moses Maimonides. Illustrated by Jeff Hill. Mount Vernon, N. Y.: Peter Pauper Press [c. 1963].

MELBER, JEHUDA
The Universality of Maimonides. New York: Jonathan David [c. 1968].

MINKIN, JACOB SAMUEL
The World of Moses Maimonides, with selections from his writings. New York: T. Yoseloff, [1957].

ROSENTHAL, GILBERT S.
Maimonides; his wisdom for our time; selected from his twelfth-century classics. Edited, newly translated, and with an introduction by Gilbert S. Rosenthal. New York: Funk and Wagnalls [c. 1969].

SPERO, SHUBERT
The Faith of a Jew; Selections from Moses ben Maimon (Rambam). New York: Spero Foundation, 1949. (Jewish Pocket Books, No. 12). Selections from the, so-called, non-rationalistic elements in the writings of Maimonides.

Selected Bibliography

TWERSKY, ISADORE

A Maimonides Reader. Edited, with introductions and notes by Isadore Twersky. New York, Behrman House, 1972.

C. WORKS ABOUT MAIMONIDES

1. Collective Volumes.

BARON, SALO W., ed.

Essays on Maimonides, an octocentennial volume, edited by Salo Wittmayer Baron...New York: Columbia University Press, 1941. "The addresses given at the celebration held under the auspices of Columbia University [1956] and the essays...written shortly thereafter... appear without any substantive alteration."— Pref.

Contents: The celebration of the 800th anniversary of the birth of Moses Maimonides, Casa de las Españas, Columbia University, March 30, 1935: Introduction by N. M. Butler, Chairman. Moses Maimonides, the philosopher, by Richard McKeon.—Maimonides, the scientist, by Richard Gottheil.—Maimonides, the leader and law-giver, by S. W. Baron.—Homage to Maimonides, by Étienne Gilson.—The literary character of the *Guide for the Perplexed,* by Leo Strauss.—Maimonides' Treatise on Resurrection; — a comparative study, by Joshua Finkel. — A Responsum of Maimonides, by

Selected Bibliography

Richard Gottheil.—The economic view of Maimonides, by S. W. Baron.—The medical work of Maimonides, by Max Meyerhof. — Index. (Reprinted: New York, AMS Press, 1968).

EPSTEIN, ISIDORE, ed.
Moses Maimonides, 1136-1204. Anglo-Jewish Papers in connection with the Eighth Centenary of his birth. Edited by I. Epstein. London: The Soncino Press, [1935].

Contents: Moses Maimonides: A general estimate, by J. H. Hertz. — Maimonides' sources and his method in H. Taanith, I. 17, by Adolph Büchler. — Maimonides conception of the law and the ethical trend of his Halachah, by I. Epstein. — The union of prophetism and philosophism in the thought of Maimonides, by R. V. Feldman. — Maimondies as halachist, by I. Herzog. — The place of Maimonides' Mishneh Torah in the history and development of the Halachah, by A. Marmorstein.

2. General Works.

BOKSER, BEN ZION
The Legacy of Maimonides, New York: Hebrew Publishing Co., 1962.

BRATTON, FRED GLADSTONE
Maimonides Medieval Modernist. Boston: Beacon Press, (c. 1967).

Selected Bibliography

The author, a Christian scholar wrote this work "so it may be that a non-Jewish approach to the life and teachings of the Rambam can bring the subject a greater degree of objectivity and a wider perspective."

MUENZ, ISAAC
Maimonides (the Rambam). The story of his life and genius; translated from the German, with an introduction by Henry T. Schnittkind. Octocentennial edition. Boston: Winchell-Thomas Co., 1935.

ROTH, LEON
The Guide for the Perplexed: Moses Maimonides. London: Hutchinson's University Library, [1948].

SARACHEK, JOSEPH
Faith and Reason; the conflict over the rationalism of Maimonides. Williamsport, Bayard Press, 1935. (Reprinted: New York, Hermon Press, 1970.)

SILVER, DANIEL JEREMY
Maimonidean Criticism and the Maimonidean Controversy, 1180-1240. Leiden: E. J. Brill, 1965.

ZEITLIN, SOLOMON
Maimonides; a biography. New York: Bloch Publishing Co., 1965.

ILLUSTRATIONS

PORTRAIT OF MAIMONIDES *Frontispiece*

This portrait has been reproduced from a photograph
newly made from Ugolinus, *Thesaurus Anti-
quitatum Sacrarum*, Venice, 1744, vol. i., p.
ccclxxxiv. As to the authenticity of the portrait
nothing is known. Dr. A. Benisch quotes the
following communication from Reggio to S.
Stern : " In the celebrated work *Thesaurus*,
&c., is found the likeness of Maimonides, which
the author says was taken *ex antiqua tabula*.
(See scroll encircling the picture.) Ugolinus,
however, does not state more fully or circum-
stantially how he came into possession of this
tabula, where it existed, and whether any one
bore testimony to the authenticity of the likeness. However, as Ugolinus is known as an
industrious, honourable man, acquainted with
his subject, and as he cannot readily be suspected of fraud, there is nothing against the
probability that when his work was published,
he really had before him such a tabula " (Benisch, Maimonides, note 32). This may well
be true, yet the portrait cannot, without further
evidence, be accepted as authentic. But as it
possesses some antiquarian interest, and has now
become accepted in several works as the conventional portrait of Maimonides, it was thought
best to reproduce it here, from a fresh photograph by Mr. W. H. Hayles of Cambridge.

Illustrations

THE MOSQUE AT CORDOVA

To face page 8

The Cordova Mosque, now the Cathedral, was designed by Abd-er-Rahman I. at the close of the
eighth century. It was converted into a Cathedral when Ferdinand of Castile gained possession of the city in 1236. "The exterior, with
the straight lines of its square buttress towers,
has a heavy and somewhat ungainly appearance ; but the interior is one of the most beautiful specimens of Moorish architecture in
Europe." The Mosque occupied a high rank
for sanctity, being by many Mohammedans
placed third after the Kaaba at Mecca and the
Mosque of Omar in Jerusalem. The central
vista of pillars is shown in this picture. There
were originally 1200 monolithic columns ; of
these about 700 now remain. "Passing through
a grand courtyard about 500 feet in length,
shady with palm and cypress and orange
trees, and fresh with the full flow of fountains,
the visitor enters a magnificent and bewilder-
ing labyrinth of pillars. Porphyry and jasper,
and marbles of many a tint, are boldly combined in a matchless mosaic." These pillars
were derived from various sources. Some are
said to be Roman, taken from the Temple of
Janus, the site of which the Mosque is believed
to occupy. Not many Roman remains are
otherwise extant in the city. Cordova, probably a Carthaginian foundation, became a
Roman Colony at about the year 150 B.C. In
the time of Strabo it was still the largest city
in Spain. Under the Goths it maintained its
importance, and its Bishop, Hosius, presided
at the Council of Nice. The Moors made Cordova the capital, of their Spanish dominions,
and much enhanced its beauty. Since the
beginning of the thirteenth century the city has
steadily declined. The Roman remains were
destroyed in the Middle Ages by Moors and
Spaniards alike. In modern times the city has

Illustrations

never recovered from the ravages of the French
army under Dupont in 1808. But the Mosque
still enshrines the ancient history of Cordova.
For, some of the columns which still stand came
" from the spoils of Nîmes or Narbonne, part
from Seville or Tarragona, some from the older
ruins of Carthage, and others as a present to
Abd-er-Rahman from Leo of Byzantium."

SARACEN *MESHREBIYAS* *To face page* 48

This picture is from a photograph taken by F. Frith
some half century back. There are few houses
of the kind now in Cairo, for Mehemet Ali
ordered the demolition of the lattices owing to
the prevalence of fires. The lattices, or *meshrebiyas*, are a characteristic feature of Saracen
architecture.

" One charming feature of the exterior of a Cairo
house is the *meshrebiya* of delicate turned
tracery. There is no reason to doubt that this
kind of work is very old, but whether by reason
of its fragility or the frequent conflagrations that
afflicted the city, no ancient examples have been
preserved. The few wooden lattices that still
remain in the older mosques are of quite a different style. . . . The name (*meshrebiya*) is derived from the root which means *to drink* (which
occurs in *sherbet*), and is applied to lattice windows because the porous water-bottles are often
placed in them to cool. Frequently there is a
semi-circular niche projecting out of the middle
of the lattice for the reception of a *kulla*, or
carafe. The delicately turned knobs and balls,
by which the patterns of the lattice-work are
formed, are sufficiently near together to conceal
whatever passes within from the inquisitive eyes
of opposite neighbours, and yet there is enough
space between them to allow free access of air.
A *meshrebiya* is, indeed, a cooling-place for
human beings as well as water-jars, and at once
a convent-grating and a spying-place for the
women of the *harim*, who can watch their Love-

Illustrations

lace through the meshes of the windows without being seen in return. Yet there are convenient little doors that open in the lattice-work, if the inmates choose to be seen even as they see ; and the fair ladies of Cairo are not always above the pardonable vanity of letting a passer-by discover that they are fair" (Stanley Lane-Poole, " The Story of Cairo," Dent, 1902, pp. 11, 285). The *meshrebiyas* have now given place to Italian *persiennes ;* but in Frith's time Cairo contained many of these beautiful structures of Saracen design, one of which is here reproduced.

RICHARD I. AND SALADIN
To face page 112

This picture represents one of the fierce conflicts between Richard I. and Saladin in Palestine, during Richard's famous march along the coast. The battle of Arsuf, which led to the capture of Ascalon, September 7, 1191, is here depicted. The Crusaders won a complete victory. The illustration is from a painting by Abraham Cooper (1787-1868). " As a painter of battle-pieces, Cooper stands pre-eminent " (" Dictionary of National Biography," vol. xii., p. 110). The picture is reproduced by kind permission of Messrs. Graves, Pall Mall, London.

"THE GUIDE OF THE PERPLEXED"
To face page 128

Facsimile, reduced, of a page of the author's autograph of the "Guide of the Perplexed"(Arabic). There are two leaves (four sides) of this MS. now in Cambridge (Taylor-Schechter Collection). Full facsimiles of the four pages are given by Dr. H. Hirschfeld in the *Jewish Quarterly Review*, vol. xv. The passage here given is from Part I. chap. lxiv., and the last ten lines were intensified on the print before reproduction.

Illustrations

AUTOGRAPHS . . *To face page* 160

Three reduced facsimiles are here given from autographs of Maimonides.

(1) Portion of an autograph letter in Arabic. The
original MS. was brought from Cairo by Dr.
Schechter, and is now in the University Library,
Cambridge (Taylor-Schechter Collection).

(2) Autograph " Response " (Arabic) to a question
addressed to Maimonides on the subject of a
teacher of girls in Cairo. The question and
answer show that " the education of girls was
not entirely neglected in Egypt " in Maimonides'
day. See the article by the Rev. G. Margoliouth in the *Jewish Quarterly Review*, vol. xi.,
p. 533, where the full facsimile is given. The
original is now in the British Museum.

(3) Hebrew note by Maimonides at the end of a
MS. of Part II. of the *Yad Hachazaka*. The
note indicates that this codex had been revised
from the author's private copy of his work.
The MS. is in the Bodleian Library, Oxford.
A full page facsimile is given in Dr. Neubauer's
Portfolio of " Facsimiles of Hebrew MSS. in
the Bodleian Library," Oxford, 1886, Plate IV.

Moses Maimonides

CHAPTER I

Early Years in Cordova

1135–1148

THE Cordova in which Maimonides was born on Passover Eve 1135 was still the "Bride of Andalusia." But her spiritual charms had faded. In form she was as fair as when Abd-er-Rahman III. had made her the pride of a Spanish Khalifate which rivalled and excelled the glories of Bagdad. The city of the first Omeyyad seems to have been at least ten miles in length. "The banks of the Guadalquivir," says Mr. S. Lane-Poole,[1] "were bright with marble houses, mosques and gardens, in which the rarest flowers and trees of other countries were carefully cultivated, and the Arabs introduced their system of irrigation, which the

A

Spaniards, both before and since, have never equalled." Ez-Zahra was to Cordova what Daphne had been to Antioch under the Seleucids. The Moors were the spiritual heirs of the Hellenists; in their scheme of life all the faculties of body and soul were organically united. It is hard to judge the Cordova of old by its tawdry ruins of to-day. But the Great Mosque is still the wonder and delight of sightseers. Much of its beauty still remains. "Travellers stand amazed among the forest of columns, which open out in apparently endless vistas on all sides. The porphyry, jasper and marbles are still in their places; the splendid glass mosaics, which artists from Byzantium came to make, still sparkle like jewels on the walls; the daring architecture of the sanctuary, with its fantastic crossed arches, is still as imposing as ever; the courtyard is still leafy with the orange-trees that prolong the vistas of columns. As one stands before the loveliness of the great mosque, the thought goes back to the days of the glories of Cordova, the palmy days of the Great Khalif, which will never return."

If Cordova to-day, after ravaging centuries of strife and neglect, retains so much of her external comeliness, imagination easily brings back to us the impression which she must have made on a bright Jewish boy in the

first half of the twelfth century. Maimonides
was no poet, and he has left no record of his
feelings. But, even when days of persecution
dawned, he clung to Spain with a tenacity
born of intense admiration and affection. The
medieval Jewish poets write of the cities of
Spain with an enthusiasm and tenderness such
as no other city but Jerusalem ever evoked
from the Hebraic muse. One may search in
vain, in the writings of ancient Jews, with the
exception of Philo, for any similar eulogies
of the Seleucid or Lagid centres of Hellenism.
The origin of this love is simple. The Moor
was Hebraic in his pure monotheism, his stern
purpose, his devotion to the righteous ideals
of life ; he was Hellenic in his graces, in his
culture. His Hellenism made him tolerant,
his Hebraism imparted to him profundity.
Thus, in her youth Cordova had been fair
in mind as in form, and a noble soul had
looked out from her alluring eyes. Not
quenched, yet sadly dimmed, was this love-
light, when Maimonides was born in the city,
renowned for its manufactures, its arts, its
schools, and its famous men. Cordova was
the birthplace of Lucan, Seneca, and Averroes.
In Abd-er-Rahman's days Cordova was the
home of European culture. Poetry was
innate in her people, and sweet songs were
improvised by statesmen on their divans and

3

by boatmen as they passed under the noble bridge whose seventeen arches still span the "mighty stream" (Guadalquivir).

The combination of political sagacity and devotion to the muses cannot be bequeathed. It is the rare possession of rulers such as Marcus Aurelius, and though it has been more often found in eastern monarchs, yet it is a personal possession, not an heirloom. The entail is for a single life. Abd-er-Rahman's son inherited one side only of his father's composite character. He was a bookman, not a statesman. He had no power to control the mixed races over whom he ruled. The failure of Islam as a conquering force is written in that last phrase. At no time was a Mohammedan host homogeneous in race or ideals. United under the stress of battle, the parts dissolved in the calm of victory. In Andalusia, what the khalifs lacked was for a brief space supplied by the Vizir Almanzor, merciless, subtle, "victorious by the grace of God." When Almanzor died, and, as the monk said, "was buried in hell," Andalusia fell a prey to factions. For nearly a century the country was "torn to pieces by jealous chiefs, aggressive and quarrelsome tyrants, Moors, Arabs, Slavs and Spaniards." One puppet khalif succeeded another, and revolution followed revolution, varying only in

4

horror. The Christians of the north were not slow to take their advantage. The Christian reconquest of Spain had, in fact, begun on the morrow after Roderick's defeat and death in 711. The victory of Charles Martel at Tours in 732 had for ever stayed the stream of Mohammedan conquest in Western Europe. The Moors in Spain retained what Tarik had won, but their hold was weakened just when their foes grew stronger.

Alfonso VI. and the Cid were carrying all before them when a new influence made itself felt. From Northern Africa had come the original conquerors of the Goths, and from the same region were now summoned the Berber saints, the Almoravids, under Yussuf son of Teshfin. The second khalif of this dynasty, Ali (1106-1143), sat on the throne of Cordova when Maimonides was born. Valiant and uncouth, fitter for camp than for court, Yussuf again led the Crescent to victory. The Cid died in 1099, and Mohammedan Spain, Toledo excepted, became a province of the great African empire of the Almoravids. "The reign of the Puritans had come, and without a Milton to soften its austerity." Worse still, the Puritanism was unreal. The savage Berbers had no appreciation for the poets and

savants who had previously basked in the
royal favour. But they also lost their martial
bearing, their manly endurance; they seized
upon the material luxuries of Cordova without
absorbing her refinement of ideals. Their
very tolerance was weakness. It needed the
fanaticism of another African, Abdullah-ibn-
Tumart, to rouse the Moors once more to a
fiercer courage and a deeper, if more persecut-
ing, piety. Till that happened between 1145
and 1148 the country was worse off than it
had been under the smaller tyrants from
whom Yussuf had freed it. The Castilians
resumed their raids into Andalusia, and under
Alfonzo the Battler in 1133 the resolute
Christian invaders burned the very suburbs
of Cordova.

The internal fortunes of the Jews had
shared none of these fluctuations. Steadily
Cordova replaced the Babylonian cities of
Sora and Pumbaditha as the headquarters of
Jewish learning and authority. The centre
of gravity of Judaism passed from Asia to
Europe. The Jews of Andalusia enjoyed
no monotony of sunshine, but having once
realised the saving power of a Judaism allied
to culture, the Spanish Jews never abandoned
the ideal. On the eve of their expulsion from
Spain in 1492 their leader was just such
another man as Chasdai had been in the

6

tenth, and as Samuel the Nagid (Prince) had
been in the eleventh century. Isaac Abarbanel well rounded off the line begun by
Chasdai-ibn-Shaprut. The Moors had established a régime to which they were themselves
faithless, but the Jews were loyal to it unto
death. The Jews did not abandon or change
their own ideals; they re-framed their own old
picture, they acquired a new setting for their
own priceless jewel. Judaism was not dependent for its vitality on Moor or Spaniard. In
Germany and in France movements were
already in progress which were destined to
survive and control the Spanish influences on
Judaism. But the fulness of life, represented
by such names as ibn Gabirol, Jehuda Halevi,
and Abraham-ibn-Ezra on the one hand, and
Chasdai, Samuel the Nagid, and Abarbanel
on the other, cannot be matched outside
Spain. And the greatest of them all, the
highest representative of the type, was
Maimonides.

At one o'clock in the afternoon of March
30 (Nisan 14), 1135, Moses, son of Maimon,
was born in Cordova. The very hour of
his birth was thus treasured up in the loving
memory of posterity. His genealogy has
been traced to Judah, the Prince, compiler
of the Mishnah, and through him to the
royal house of David. It is at least certain

that he came of a family of scholars. He
himself has recorded a modest yet honourable pedigree, describing himself as Moses,
son of Maimon, *dayan* (official Rabbi or
"judge"), son of the learned R. Joseph,
son of R. Isaac, *dayan*, son of R. Joseph,
dayan, son of R. Obadiah, *dayan*, son of
R. Solomon, son of R. Obadiah.[2] Of the
boyhood of Moses we know little. Legend has been busy with him, and the story
goes that the child revealed but little of the
man. But the contrast thus drawn between
the dull, idle lad and the brilliant, industrious
2.* man is unfounded. The father, Maimon
(*i.e.* Felix, Benedictus or Baruch), was a
scholar and a man of enlightenment, Talmudist, astronomer and mathematician. Maimon (or Maimûn) was a disciple of Joseph
Ibn Migash (1077–1141), who had imbibed
the spirit of Alfassi and who had succeeded the
latter as head of the school at Lucena. The
poet, Jehuda Halevi, eulogised Ibn Migash
in lavish terms, but the eulogy was well
deserved. Maimon profited by his studies
under this renowned teacher, composed commentaries on the Talmud, a work on the
ritual, and expository notes on the Pentateuch. He influenced his son's mind pro-
foundly, but in one respect father and child
differed. "The son was not unemotional,

8

but he was a philosopher first of all. The father is all enthusiasm, full of faith, longing to dwell in the beautiful stories of Hagadah, not afraid of believing in angels, not desirous of making God an abstraction, or the apostle of God merely a deep thinker." He was gifted with a genius for allegory, and his images flow like a soothing stream over the reader's heart. His most famous work, the " Letter of Consolation," must have bound up many a wound, and filled with fresh courage those who despairingly feared that God had forsaken His world.

His son Moses grew up in this gentle and refined home, his mind and soul trained by a father who, amid the tribulations which were soon to follow, was upheld by the same confidence and trust which he sought to impart to others. Maimon's precept and example planted in his son's heart a pure and ineradicable veneration for all the tried and traditional virtues of the Jewish character. The Law and the Commandments were his delight. Not the less was this so because Maimon at the same time instilled into him a powerful inclination towards science and philosophy. In Maimon's home the stream of life ran broad and deep. What was Jewish, what was human, alike found a resting-place in the capacious soul of Maimonides. The

Talmud was his chosen love. The works of Alfassi and of Ibn Migash were the eyes with which he penetrated into the Rabbinical lore. Equally devoted was the young scholar to the various sciences expounded by ancient Greeks, medieval Arabs, and Hebrews of all ages. Mathematics, philology, natural science, medicine, logic, and metaphysics, were included in the liberal education of the day, and all of these were the familiar friends of our hero's early manhood. Through the maze of these varied pursuits his keen, orderly intellect found a clear and straight path. Knowledge was not with him a more or less confused amalgam of discordant or dissociated elements : it was one and indivisible. And he early learned the lesson, most precious to the genuine student, that " it is possible for a wise man to be taught by a fool." He saw the limitations of astrology, for instance, but he recognised the necessity of mastering its literature.

But not only in the acquisition and ordering of facts, in the awakening and development of his great intellect, did the youthful Moses grow under the hand of his father Maimon. In this formative period his character received the bent which marked it throughout life. Faith and Reason, simple piety and fearless inquiry, saintly self-aban-

3.*

donment to God and free examination of
ethical sanctions and religious dogmas —
these which are commonly opposites were
blended in him into an inseparable unity.
He was *perfect* with his God. He was
faithful to the Law of God as revealed in
Scripture, and to the divine reason present
in the human soul. He was true to the
spirit of Judaism when he announced as the
fundamental formula of his life the memor-
able imperative : " Know the God of thy
father and serve Him." The tradition which
binds the ages together, father to son, as
knowers and servers of the same, changeless,
eternal God is expressed in the phrase : " God
of *thy father*." But something more is also
conveyed. Knowledge and service : not obedience with blind eyes, not disobedience with
penetrative gaze ; but open-eyed obedience
and service. An earnest sense that he was
born to teach this truth to his own age and
to posterity seems early to have forced itself
upon him. It filled him with strenuous purpose, but it softened while it strengthened
him. Not less of him than of Hillel could
it be said that his gentleness, his even temper,
his modesty, were as conspicuous as his belief
in himself and his mission, his giant - like
intellect, his determination to make the truth
prevail.

CHAPTER II

The Unitarian Persecution

1148-1159

THE culture of the Almoravids was superficial, but the reaction which it provoked was deep-rooted. A profound suspicion roused to frenzy a new sect of Mohammedans who, like so many of other races and creeds then and since, saw in ethics the foe of æsthetics, and fancied that refinement of manners is synonymous with laxity of life. The Puritan movement in Islam had its origin and its headquarters in Northern Africa. When, in due course, the movement won its way to Spain, Andalusia was governed from Morocco. Hence the " Unitarians " (Almohades)—as the Puritans were called—obtained no real hold on Spain, and in 1212 the disastrous field of Las Navas decided their fate for ever. The intervening half century, during which the Almohades were supreme, was fraught with momentous consequence for Maimonides. The early trials to which he was subjected, the enforced change of domicile, the critical situations, saved him from becoming a mere philosophical recluse. He became a statesman as well as an author, a statesman not in the sense that he ever held a diplomatic post or wielded political power, but in the sense that his thought was brought into close relation with the real affairs of life. He was not a " man of the world," but his enduring influence may be traced in part to his large-minded deference to the actuality of things. His mind moved in the world of men, not in a mystic world of its own. His rough contact with men made of the foremost Jewish metaphysician of the middle ages the most practical codifier of Jewish law and custom. The midday sun rather than the midnight lamp shines through all his work.

The founder of the Unitarian sect was Abdallah-ibn-Tumart, a man of great spiritual and personal magnetism, inspired at once by religious enthusiasm and political ambition. He conceived an Islam both pure and powerful ; simple in the life it inculcated, world-wide in its dominion. The Koran and the sword, when both are forcibly wielded, make the most terrible combination that human history has ever witnessed. Ibn Tumart must not,

however, be mistaken for an ignorant fanatic.
Warring against luxury in living and dress,
against poetry, music and painting, his doctrine
was a highly metaphysical expression of ab-
stract Monotheism. The "Unitarian"
Confession of Faith has been preserved and
it is necessary to cite it. The document
illustrates the danger which ever threatens a
spiritual Monotheism, the danger of becoming
Pantheistic. It also helps to explain how
Jews during the Unitarian persecution could
easily accept Islam as the price of their life or
security, and further, how it happened that
Jewish public opinion could regard such
apostasy as involving no disgrace. The
Moslem belief in the Unity of God was as
uncompromising as the Jewish, and in Ibn
Tumart's expression of it was even freer from
anthropomorphic suggestions. Had Judaism
merely consisted of certain dogmas or formulæ,
it is hard to see what could have enabled the
Jews "to withstand the temptations to become
followers of the Apostle of God in the latter
half of the twelfth century." The following
is Ibn Tumart's "Confession," [3] which has
some striking points of similarity with the
medieval Synagogue Hymn of *Adon Olam* :—

In the name of God, the Most Merciful, the
Most Gracious. May Allah lead us and you in
the right path. Know ye, then, that it is absolutely

necessary for every Moslem to know that God, be he magnified and extolled, is One in his kingdom ; that he is the creator of the whole Universe, the heights and depths, the throne, the heavens and the earth and all that is in them, and all that is between them. All creation is subject to his power. Not a mote is moved unless with his permission. He has no counsellor in his kingdom, no associate in the work of his creation. He is living and ever-existing. To him appertaineth not slumber or sleep. He knoweth that which is hidden and that which is seen. Nought on earth or in heaven is concealed from him. He knoweth that which is on dry land and that which is in the sea. Not a leaf falls to the ground unless he knows it, not a single grain in the darkest parts of the earth, neither a green thing nor a dry thing, that is not written in his clear book. He comprehends all things with his knowledge. He counts all things according to their number. He doeth all that he desireth. He hath power over all that he wisheth to perform. To him is the kingdom, to him belongeth wealth. To him is power and might. To him appertaineth eternity. To him belongeth judgment. He maketh his decrees. To him belong praise and adoration. To him belong the best names.[4] None can hinder that which he decrees. None can prevent that which he ordains. He doeth in his creation that which he desires. He hopes for no reward and fears no punishment. He is subject to no decree, to no judgment. All his favours to us are acts of grace. Every punishment he inflicts upon us is just. None can say to him: What doest thou? but we can be asked as to our deeds. He was before all creation. Of him we cannot attribute any direction in space. He is not above us nor below us, not at our right hand nor at our left, not before us nor at our back. The words whole and part are inapplicable to him. It cannot be said whence he came or whither he goeth, or how he existeth. He is the former of space, the ordainer of time. Time does not contain him. Space does not hold him. No intelligence can grasp him, no intellect can comprehend him. No imagination can characterise him. No soul can form an image of his likeness. Nothing is like unto him. But still he hears and he sees. He is the tenderest of rulers, the most loving of helpers. Those who know him know him through his works; but they deny all limit to his greatness. However our imagination may conceive God, he the Exalted is different from our conception of him.

The moral reformation, dignified by this pure Monotheism, spread rapidly in North-West Africa. When Ibn Tumart died, his disciple Abdulmumen was recognised as the Emir al-Mumenin, "Prince of the Faithful." Victory after victory was won, and the dynasty of the Almoravids was uprooted. The reformers were as intolerant of other religions as they were of sectarianism in Islam. No

Church and no Synagogue was the battle-cry of the Almohades. When Morocco fell into Abdulmumen's hands after a prolonged siege (1146), Christians and Jews were fellows in misfortune. To both was offered the alternative of death or apostasy. Under considerable pressure Abdulmumen so far modified his edict as to permit heretics to emigrate. Many availed themselves of the opportunity; but while the Christians were able to find an asylum in Northern Spain, no such refuge was open to the mass of the Jews. Many suffered martyrdom, but the majority assumed the disguise of Islam, hoping for better times. Fanatic as the Almohades were, they were much less skilful than the Inquisition subsequently proved itself in the matter of assuring the complete surrender of converts. To accept Monotheism, to profess belief in the prophetic inspiration of Mohammed, to attend the Mosque on rare occasions, this constituted all that was expected of them. "In private, however, they practised the Jewish rites in all their details, as the Almohades employed no police spies to observe the action of the converts."

Two years later the Unitarians invaded Andalusia, and Cordova fell into their hands (May or June 1148). The magnificent synagogues were destroyed. In Spain the Jews had developed an ecclesiastical art, inspired by Moorish models and originating in the same cause. In Islam art is invariably associated with architecture. The Jews in Spain were secure enough under Islamic rule to venture on ambitious architectural schemes. Now the choicest products of this art fell before the ruthless Puritans. The schools, too, at Seville and Lucena were dismantled. It seemed as though the splendid edifice of Jewish scholarship erected by Samuel the Nagid and Isaac Alfassi was doomed to destruction. In Germany the Jews had already sunk to the position of body-slaves of the Emperor. In Northern France Rabbenu Tam had left no equal successor. The Provençal schools had not yet produced original masters, and the eminence of Toledo in Christian Spain was still to come. No one yet realised that, in the person of Maimonides, Spain in its hour of need had given birth to the man. Yet, unlike their brethren in Northern Africa, the great mass of Andalusian Jews refused to conform to the demands of the Almohades. A few offered lip-allegiance to Mohammed, but most preferred exile to apostasy even in outward show. Maimon belonged to the sterner group.[5] He cast no stones at the weaker brethren, but himself refused to bow down in the House of Rimmon.

With his family he wandered hither and thither for several years, at first perhaps settling in Port Almeria, but forced to retire thence when the Almohades captured the place in 1151. For eight or nine years we lose trace of Maimon, but we know that he remained in Spain without a permanent home or a settled position.

The young son of Maimon never, amid all these distractions, swerved from his ideals. In this formative period he laid the foundation of that mastery over the Rabbinical literature which he subsequently possessed to a unique extent. As he could not carry many books with him on his journeys, he was forced to make his memory his library, and to rely on his own stores. The Babylonian Talmud was not yet thoroughly interpreted; nor had the admirable commentaries of Rashi found their way from France to Spain. The scholars of the earlier middle ages, the "Geonim," had, as Maimonides himself writes, "made fitful attempts to explain the Talmud, but none of them wrote a complete commentary, some being prevented by death, others by lack of leisure." Maimonides himself was destined to a similar fate. He designed a commentary on the whole Talmud, but his plan was not fully realised. Still he made much progress during this unsettled period of his life. He prosecuted his researches into the extant works of the Geonim, and collected the notes of his father and of his father's teacher, his own chosen model, Joseph Ibn Migash. He originated besides collating. His practical bent at once revealed itself, for he commenced with those sections of the Talmud in which predominates the *halachah* (practical law) applicable to his own and to all times. Before he was twenty-three years of age he had finished his notes on many tractates (*massechtoth*) of the "Orders" (*sedarim*) Moed (Festivals), Nashim (Laws of Marriage, &c.), and Nezikin (civil and criminal law), and on the tractate Chullin (dietary laws). He explained the Talmud not word by word but in running paraphrase, often prefixing a statement of the general principle on which the Talmudic discussion was based. He made no display of painful ingenuity in meeting difficulties, but frankly confessed : "I do not see how to explain this matter." The Rabbi of old had counselled : " Teach thy tongue to say, I do not know," and both Rashi and Maimonides in their modest self-confidence were conspicuous in their obedience to this ancient advice. Besides this commentary on the Babylonian Talmud, Maimonides set himself to extract the practical *halachah* from the Talmud of

The Unitarian Persecution

Jerusalem, doing for the latter less-studied work what Alfassi had done for its better-known counterpart.   4.*

But the Talmud, though the first and chief object of Maimonides' devotion, was not his only love. Among his early works was a short treatise on the Jewish Calendar (*Maamar ha-ibbur*).[6] This displayed no originality, but was a clear, scientific, systematic survey, written in Hebrew in 1158 in response to a request from a friend. Already his brethren were looking to him for solutions of their difficulties, and much of his more important work was similarly composed to satisfy the demands of correspondents. At about the same date he wrote a book on Logic (*Milloth Higgayon*), 6.* to which Moses Mendelssohn subsequently added a Commentary. The same year saw 7.* the initiation of the first of Maimonides' great trilogy. This was the *Commentary on the Mishnah*. In his Talmudic enterprise he had forerunners; in the new undertaking he was a pioneer.[7] The completion of the Commentary belongs to a later period of his life, but the fact that it was planned and begun in his early manhood deserves special note. "Confusion," he writes in his introduction, " besets the student of the Mishnah. Until a man has closely read the Talmudical

discussion, though he be the greatest of
Geonim, he cannot understand the Mishnah.
Now, in the Talmud, the discussion of a
single *halachah* sometimes occupies four or
five pages, for subject grows out of subject
with arguments, objections, and replies ; so
that even when the Talmud has been
mastered, the real significance of the Mishnah
can only be grasped by a student skilled in
clear thought. Moreover, for the explanation of one and the same *halachah* the reader
must often refer to two or more tractates."
The expositors of the Mishnah had previously
treated Mishnah and Talmud, text and commentary, simultaneously ; being more concerned to provide a clue to the intricacies of
the latter than a light to the simplicity of the
former. This was a grave critical mistake,
and though Maimonides did not regard the
Mishnah from any other than the Talmudic
point of view, still he realised that it was
essential to treat the Mishnah, (with which
we must include the Tannaite elements in
other Rabbinical compilations), in and for itself
if the Jewish Tradition was to be based on a
sound historical foundation. His aim was,
however, practical rather than critical. He
loved and venerated the Rabbinical dialectics,
but he felt that most men could not be expected to devote the necessary time to them.

The Unitarian Persecution

Brevity in place of prolixity, a clue to ancient mazes; to beginners an encouragement, to experts a work of reference, to all a better understanding of the tradition, and with it a release of the student's time and thought for other occupations besides the dialectics of the schools. This point will recur subsequently, and it will be necessary to discuss the extent to which Maimonides succeeded, and the inwardness of the opposition which his motives aroused. The *Siraj* or " Light " (*Maor*), for so the Commentary on the Mishnah was named, was not completed till 1168. But, as indicated above, it was begun in Spain. In the final words to the *Siraj* he refers to the conditions under which he started. "While my mind was ever troubled amid the God-decreed expatriations from one end of heaven to the other, I wrote notes on many an *halachah* on journeys by land, or while tossed on the stormy waves at sea." The latter phrase seems to refer to the voyages undertaken when he left Spain, and when subsequently he escaped from Fez. We must now follow him on his fortunes in various lands, until in 1165 he found a final home in the city about to become Saladin's Cairo.

CHAPTER III

Life in Fez

1160–1165

AFTER enduring for more than ten years the perils and discomforts of a wandering life, Maimon resolved to emigrate from Spain.[8] Taking with him his daughter, his two sons Moses and David, he sailed for the Maghreb, "the Land of the West," and settled in Fez. Maimon and David engaged in commerce, while Moses devoted himself to his studies in theology and medicine. Maimon's motive for selecting Morocco as his new abode cannot be clearly ascertained. Fez was under the same rule as Cordova, and a "Moslem state for Moslems" was the watchword of the Unitarians in Africa as well as in Spain. There were parts of Christian Europe in which Maimon might have found a tolerant if not a friendly reception. The saintly influence of Bernard of Clairvaux did not fade away when this "oracle of Europe" died in 1153. The second Crusade had been, on the whole, productive of a better feeling between the devotees of Church, Mosque, and Synagogue. But Maimon had grown old in a Moorish society, and would have felt himself a stranger to the language and habits of a Christian community. He had another reason for choosing Fez as his home. Neither he nor his son was personally known to the Mohammedan scientists of Morocco. Hence they would not be driven into the category of ordinary *anusim*, pseudo-converts to Islam under pressure of *force majeure*. They were not known as Jews to the local authorities, but in all probability they were commonly assumed to be Moslems. The evidence does not justify us in asserting that Maimonides ever did more than act a part of tacit consent, though he has been suspected of a more positive conformity. That he joined in the *Tarawih* prayers during the month of Ramadan, or made any other serious ritual concessions to Islam, is improbable in itself, and is certainly not supported by adequate testimony.[9]

In a certain sense, the dual life that Maimonides passed in Fez chimed in well with the needs of his intellectual development. His close intercourse with Jewish scholars satisfied his eager desire for the further acquisition of Rabbinical learning, and his intimate acquaintance with Moslem literati stimulated his interest in science and philosophy. In Judah ha-Kohen Ibn Shoshan, head of the Jewish community in Fez, he found a companion and guide in his researches into Jewish lore. During the five years passed in the Maghreb he made considerable progress with his Commentary on the Mishnah. On the other hand, he frequently refers in his later medical treatises to the experience gained among the Moslems of the Maghreb. The Unitarians (Almohades) were not foes to enlightenment. It is true that Ibn Tumart assailed the Moravid Khalif because his daughter appeared in public unveiled, because wine was drunk in defiance of the Koran, and the flesh of swine was offered for sale in open market. Yet the metaphysical tone of Ibn Tumart's *Tauhid*, or formula of/Unity (p. 14 above), would have led us to expect that the new Puritanism was compatible with a genuine regard for science and philosophy. "There is no Church and no Synagogue in our land" ran the Moslem boast, but the vaunt did not add, "and there is no school." Well-known facts tally with this inference. "A man like Ibn Tofail, the author of the philosophical

romance, *Hai ben Jokdan*, which has been
translated into Hebrew, Latin, Dutch, and
English, and a man like Averroes during an
important part of his life, flourished at the
Court of the Almohades, though the latter in
the end was banished." [10]

The double life of the ordinary Jew of
Fez was not, however, without its dangers.
Maimonides and the leaders of thought might
remain absolutely true to their religious covenant, but commoner men could not but suffer
from a continued yielding of lip-homage to
Mohammed, occasionally supplemented by
compulsory visits to the mosques, at which
hymns and sermons were devoted to eulogy
of the Prophet. Some of the Maghreb Jews
began to persuade themselves that Islam was
a God-sent substitute for Judaism, and that
Mohammed had been born to replace Moses.
It was to meet this danger that Maimon
composed the "Letter of Consolation" to
which reference has been made in a previous
chapter.

Maimon's Letter was written in Arabic in
1159 or 1160.[11] The author argues that
Israel's tribulations were a chastisement of
love, the tender correction administered by a
father to his wayward child, not the desola-
ting vengeance of a potentate against a re-
bellious favourite. Let no Israelite imagine

27

that God had changed His plan, that Israel, His beloved son, is now cast off for another. "God does not desire a thing and then despise it; he does not favour and then reject." Where is the other religion in the midst of whose camp the divine Shechina patently dwells, where are the signs and the miracles? Maimonides was not at one with his father here; his confidence in Judaism was independent of miracles.[12] Maimon makes a stronger appeal on the basis of God's promises to Israel, which, like the Law itself, are of eternal and irresistible validity. "We must no more doubt God's promises than we doubt his existence." He urges his brethren to a whole-hearted loyalty to their God. "What health can there be for him who is not whole with his Master?" He exhorts them to find salvation in spiritual communion with God; he would have them think less of this world's charm than of life everlasting; praying regularly, using, if need be, an abridged form of the liturgy, and the Arabic language, if Hebrew were unfamiliar; content with little materially, yet hoping for much spiritually. The Law of God was a Cord "suspended from earth to heaven," a sure rescue for those who, immersed in the sea of captivity, grasped at this unbreakable means of safety. Then, with noble charity towards those of his brethren who had lost firm hold of the Cord, Maimon said, " He who clings to it with his whole hand has, doubtless, more hope than he who clings to it with but part of it, *but he who clings on with the tips of his fingers has more hope than he who lets go of it altogether.*"

Coming from a foremost champion of a " legalistic " religion, this is one of the finest expressions of tolerance which medieval literature can show. The rest of Maimon's " Letter " is intensely interesting. His object is to maintain the permanence of the Jewish law and the greatness of the original lawgiver. He launches out into an extraordinary eulogy of Moses. " His creation was the evidence of the strength of God, for God created him in the most beautiful form. The light of God was clear in his face, a light more brilliant than the sun's, for the latter light was created, whereas the light of the face of our master Moses was from the light of the glory of God, which is uncreated. How magnificent were the eyes which gave forth a light which not Michael, or Gabriel, or the holy *hayoth* could look upon ! " His body was purified like that of the angels, yet was it stronger than theirs, " for those were of light, not of flesh or of blood, or of sinew or matter." " Moses was a prophet in whom

29

was the strength of God." "If any one doubted the apostleship of Moses, his life was consumed like Korah's." Maimon freely uses Moslem phrases, and describes Abraham as "the Mahdi of God." His stress on the greatness of Moses is obviously meant "as a set-off to the greatness of Mohammed." "If the law which he promulgated had to be believed merely on account of Moses' greatness, it would still have been necessary to believe it ; how much more must we believe it when that law contains the commands of the Creator and his ordinances. Gratitude and cleaving to God are necessary, on account of him who sent and of him who was sent. And how great is the glory both of the sender and the apostle ! " Maimon concludes his remarkable epistle with a detailed commentary on the 90th Psalm, "The Prayer of Moses, the man of God." Maimon sees in this Psalm a forecast of Israel's vicissitudes. He applies it, "not so much to the shortness of life as to the shortness of God's anger, and the ultimate deliverance from captivity." With exquisite fancy he turns the phrases of that noble Psalm to the contemporary condition of his people, and utters many an impassioned note of unconquerable confidence in the future restoration of Israel to its former place in God's regard. "O God, satisfy us

in the morning of the dawn of our deliverance, and favour us with thy grace. . . .
Grant thy redemption to draw near in our days, and establish in our time that which thou hast promised us ; enlighten our darkness as thou hast assured us, and thy assurance is indeed sure. 'The Lord shall arise upon thee, and his glory shall be seen upon thee.' And so may it be God's will."

Maimon appeals throughout to sentiment, and sentiment is perhaps the best guide for an individual in such a case of conscience as presented itself to the Jews of his day. But when a community is internally lacerated by a life and death struggle, the only saving guides are reason and duty. It has been objected that while the father applied the principle of faith to the question of pretended apostasy, the son applied the principle of law. But when Maimonides took a severely legal view, he did so because he was fixing a norm for other men's conduct, not for his own. For himself he might adopt an ideal standard, but of others, speaking as the upright judge, he would require no more than the letter of the law. It is characteristic of Maimonides that he elected to participate in the solution of the difficulty just at the moment when it was placed on a practical basis. Maimonides' Let-

ter does not lack feeling ; he indulges in un-
wonted invective, but its very strength lies in
its patent repression of emotion. It appears
that a Jew of the Maghreb, possibly resident
in Fez, had applied to a foreign Rabbi for
his opinion as to the conduct of Jews who
saved their own lives and preserved their
children for Judaism by uttering the formula,
"La ilaha illa Allah, wa-Muhammad rasul
Allah."—*There is no God but Allah, and
Mohammed is the prophet of Allah.* Re-
gardless of the effect of his reply on many
thousands of his brethren, the armchair hero,
to whom the appeal had been addressed,
answered that a Jew who publicly confessed
belief in Mohammed thereby denied God,
for the Moslems were idolaters. The prayers
of such a man would find no acceptance
before God, his secret performance of all the
Jewish precepts would be futile, and he could
no longer be regarded as a Jew. The only
course for a steadfast Israelite was to accept
martyrdom rather than yield.

This opinion seems to have been widely
circulated in the Maghreb, and one can well
imagine the consternation produced by such an
epistle, "turning men back from God." Some
must have felt crushed under a burden of sin,
more must have been tempted to conform in
earnest to Islam, since they were denounced

as apostates for an insincere secession from Judaism. Maimonides could not tolerate the injustice to which the Maghreb Jews were subjected by their critic, and he felt that his own conduct had been sufficiently like that of the rest of the local Jews to warrant him to associate himself personally in the charge. He does not deny that there was something to reproach in a policy of pretended submission. There is "genuine anguish" in this passage : "God is a witness that if he who has uttered these reproaches against us had uttered many more, we should not have sought help for ourselves ; we should have said, Let us lie in our shame, and let our confusion cover us, for we have sinned against the Lord our God. We know, O God, that we have done wickedly, and had it not been insisted upon that those who pray in these times are committing a transgression, we should have been silent. But will not the ignorant, if they hear that to pray is a sin, leave off praying altogether ? " He opposed the zealot with his own weapons. He, too, appealed to precedent, and showed how in the past R. Meir and R. Eleazar had saved their lives by feigning heathenism at a time of persecution. Then Maimonides develops a view which has not had altogether salutary effects on Judaism in subsequent centuries.

"The present," he said, "differs from previous experiences. In former cases, Israelites have been called upon to transgress the Law in action. Now we are not asked to render active homage to heathenism, but only to recite an empty formula which the Moslems themselves know we utter insincerely in order to circumvent a bigot." The distinction between conformity in speech and conformity in act saved many a Jewish community from extinction, but as a general principle it is untenable, and savours too strongly of casuistry. In the application of the principle to the case immediately before him, Maimonides is, however, perfectly sound. He places himself entirely at the Talmudic standpoint. The three capital offences which, the Talmud ordains, must be avoided even at the cost of martyrdom are idolatry, unchastity and murder. "But now," continues Maimonides, "nothing of this is required. Indeed any Jew who, after uttering the Moslem formula, wishes to observe the whole 613 precepts in the privacy of his home may do so without hindrance. Nevertheless, if, even under these circumstances, a Jew surrenders his life for the sanctification of the name of God before men, he has done nobly and well, and his reward is great before the Lord. But if a man asks me : Shall I be slain or

utter the formula of Islam? I answer, Utter
the formula and live."

Thus Maimonides drew back into the fold
the weaklings whom a zealot would have cast
forth into the desert of despair. He urged
them to fortitude. He warned them against
supposing that because they had strayed from
the way of the Lord they were free to
leave the path altogether. So, too, those
who profaned the Sabbath must, he said, be
treated not with contempt and rejection, but
must be brought near and urged to reform.
But he did not counsel a continuance
of this yielding to coercion, nor justify
quietism under persecution. "The advice
I give to myself, to those I love, and
to those who ask my opinion is that we
should go forth from these places, and go
to a place where we can fulfil the Law without compulsion and without fear, and that
we should even forsake our homes and our
children, and all that we possess." Those
who remain must regard themselves as parti-
ally, but not entirely, estranged from God
so long as they are not compelled to transgress actively any of God's commandments.
Should that be demanded of them, no consideration must weigh with them, no fear of
the journey, no love for their home, but they
must forthwith depart. Maimonides has no

patience with those who would soothe their conscience by the thought that soon the Messiah must appear and lead them to Jerusalem, until which event there was nothing possible except submission.

Maimonides was about twenty-five years old when he wrote in Arabic this famous *Maamar Kiddush Hashem* ("Essay on the Sanctification of God"), known also as *Iggereth Hashemad* ("Letter concerning Apostasy").[13] It was his first incursion into public life, and it placed him at a bound among the foremost authorities of the time. Henceforward men recognised in him a leader, at once statesman and enthusiast; and they sought a secure anchorage in his steadfast common sense and piety. Like a skilful physician who accurately diagnoses his patient's symptoms, at first he soothed the sufferer, then roused him to a sense of his condition. He saved Judaism from absorption into Islam in the Maghreb by persuading the pseudo-Moslems that they had not lost their inheritance in the God of Israel; but he followed this up by urging them to abandon their duplicity and live openly and whole with God. His effort was brilliantly successful, yet its very success occasioned new though more honourable dangers. The bolder spirit that now animated the Jews of Fez could not

but translate itself into action easily detected
by the Moslems.[14] These did not sit idly by
when the genius of Judaism reasserted itself.
An inquisition was instituted. The crime of
relapsing from Islam after conversion is punish-
able in Moslem law by death. Under that
law *force majeure* is no admissible plea. Judah
Ibn Shoshan was seized and executed. For
the moment Maimonides was saved from a
similar fate by the intercession of his friend,
a Moslem poet and theologian, Abul-Arab Ibn
Moisha. But his position was so hazardous
that he resolved to leave the Maghreb.[15] In
the darkness of the night (4th Iyar = 18th
April 1165) the family went on board a vessel
bound for Palestine. For six days their
voyage was calm, but on Saturday the 24th
April a terrific storm assailed the vessel, and
shipwreck seemed imminent. Then the danger
passed, and Maimonides, after the manner of
the time, solemnly vowed that he would
annually observe the 4th and 10th of Iyar as
fast days, " and as on this occasion we were
desolate and destitute of all succour but God's,
so year by year on this day will I sit solitary,
apart from all my fellow-men, to pour out my
inmost soul before the Lord alone."

A full month was occupied by the voyage
to Acre, which was reached on Sunday night
the 16th of May (3rd Sivan). As he himself

joyously wrote : "On the 3rd of Sivan I arrived safely at Acco, and was thus rescued from apostasy." The anniversary was dedicated as a family festival, for whatever had really occurred to him in Fez, he could not but feel that his position there, amid a community of pseudo-Moslems, had been open to misconstruction. He remained in Acre for several months, recruiting his health both in body and soul, breathing in the ancient home of his people the air of freedom and sincerity. He was welcomed by the small Jewish community in what was then the chief sea-port of Palestine, and he enjoyed the close friendship of the dayan, Japhet ben Eliahu. After the autumn festivals, he decided on paying a visit to Jerusalem. He arrived in the holy city on the 17th October (6th Marcheshvan). Japhet accompanied him, and the party spent three days in visiting the sacred sites and praying at the Wailing Wall. On the Sunday (the 9th Marcheshvan) they left for Hebron, "to embrace the graves of the Patriarchs in the Cave (of Macphelah)." The 6th and 9th of Marcheshvan were likewise observed in the family of Maimonides as festive anniversaries.

Palestine at that period was in Christian hands, the second Crusade having left the general situation unchanged. But few Jews

were to be found there ; the total did not
exceed 1000 families, scattered in many cities.
They were poor in goods and in culture, and
Maimonides feared to settle in an environ-
ment which offered no intellectual comrade-
ship for him. Egypt promised a fitter field
for his energies. Famous in Jewish history
as the scene of the early career of Moses,
later celebrated as the home of Philo, Egypt
was now to receive a second Moses, who
would again kindle in that land of human and
divine marvels a light for the Jews of all the
world.

CHAPTER IV

With Saladin in Cairo

1165–1174

WHEN Maimonides reached Alexandria, the last of the Fatimid Khalifs sat on the throne of Egypt. Saladin, whose life (1138–1193) practically synchronises with that of Maimonides, had not yet come to Egypt, and it was uncertain whether the country was fated to remain in Moslem, or to fall into Christian, hands. Saladin was of Kurdish descent, and his rise was due to the service rendered by his father Ayyub to Zengy, master of Mosul. Nureddin, Zengy's son, was Saladin's immediate predecessor on the throne of Aleppo. As the Moslem hero of the second Crusade, Nureddin was second only to Saladin in fame among the champions of Islam. Ayyub's younger brother, Shirkuh, was Nureddin's most trusted general. The diplomacy of Ayyub and the military genius of Shirkuh enabled Nureddin to occupy Damascus in 1154, and to realise Zengy's dream of a Syrian empire with its capital at Damascus. Till 1164 Saladin lived in obscurity at Nureddin's court, but when Shirkuh made his famous inroads into Egypt, Saladin accompanied his uncle and soon found himself ruler of the land of the Pharaohs.[16]

The Fatimids, claiming descent from Fatima, Mohammed's daughter, had for two centuries forced their presence on the Egyptians. The Fatimids were heterodox (Shiites), the masses orthodox (Sunnites), but the khalifs of this line were powerful enough by land and sea to maintain their prestige and independence. Their luxury and their prodigality, however, eventually produced their inevitable effects. The last of the Fatimids ruled from his harem. His Vizir Shawar coquetted with the Moslems and the Franks, seeking an alliance now with Nureddin in Damascus, now with Amalric in Jerusalem. In 1164 Shirkuh invaded Egypt, "a country without *men*," as the Moslem general reported to Nureddin. It took, however, some years before the Franks abandoned their hopes of winning supremacy in Egypt. By the year 1169 Shirkuh had triumphed, but within three months of his success he died, leaving the path free for his nephew. Saladin was im-

mediately appointed Vizir, and remained
master of Egypt till the death of Nureddin
in 1174 called him from Egypt to play a
greater part in the world's drama. Saladin
deserves all the honours that have been poured
on his name by historians and romancers.
" The popular conception of his character
has not erred. Magnanimous, chivalrous,
gentle, sympathetic, pure in heart and life,
ascetic and laborious, simple in his habits,
fervently devout, and only severe in his zeal
for the faith, he has been rightly held to be
the type and pattern of Saracen chivalry."
Rarely has history shown us in rivalry two
such noble characters as Saladin and Richard
Cœur de Lion. And the same epoch presents
us with the most typical medieval product of
Judaism. Like the champions of Christianity
and Islam, but with other weapons, the Jew
Maimonides was struggling for possession of
the Mount of God.

The Jewish population of Egypt was considerable. In Alexandria, where Maimonides
remained for some time, there resided about
3000 Jewish families, in Bilbeys 3000 indi-
viduals. In El-Kahira, New Cairo, 2000
Jewish families had their home; in addition
another 1000 families were settled in Old
Cairo (Fostat or Misr). The Egyptian Jews
enjoyed almost complete freedom, and under

their own Nagid (Prince) formed a community
practically self-governed, so far as its internal
affairs were concerned. Their position closely
resembled the situation of the Jewish community in Persia. The Egyptian Nagid, like
the Exilarch at Bagdad, had extensive dis-
ciplinary powers : he appointed Rabbis and
Synagogue officials ; he could punish offenders
by fines and imprisonment. Spiritually, the
condition of the Jews was less satisfactory
than it was materially. There was little
genuine devotion to the Law, there were
few men of light and leading. Karaism was
eating deep into the communal organisation.
In the capital, the Karaites were probably for
the moment more numerous than the Rabbanites ; their political influence was certainly
stronger. The adherents of the Karaite sect,
it may be explained in passing, assumed an
attitude of opposition to the Rabbanite tradition, and sought to govern their lives by the
letter of Scripture (Kara). To the Karaites was due not the foundation but the
development of a true Hebrew philology, and
when the Bible became the battlefield of men
like Saadiah and Japhet the field was, at all
events, very thoroughly trodden. Thus biblical exegesis gained what the communal
organisation lost. There was, moreover,
much to admire in the independence and

strength of character displayed by the Karaites, but their virtues have sometimes been
exaggerated in order to deal an indirect blow
at the mass of the Jews who have remained
staunch to Rabbanism. Karaism was essentially
reactionary, for starting with a profession of
hostility to tradition it soon became itself
nothing but a tradition, lacking the historical
sanction and the fertilising spiritual vitality of
the Rabbinical tradition which it sought to
replace. The two sects were not rigidly
separated, and intermarriages took place,
sometimes on terms of very remarkable
tolerance between the contracting parties.
Still the temporary supremacy of Karaism
was a menace to the Judaism of Egypt, and
none of the services which Maimonides rendered to the cause of Judaism won him so
much approval as his success in gaining for
the Rabbanites the upper hand in Egypt.[17] He
won this victory by a policy of conciliation
and firmness. He did not interfere with the
friendly intercourse between the sects, on the
contrary he held that Karaites might be visited
in their homes, that Rabbanites might bury
their dead, comfort their mourners, and
initiate their children into the covenant of
Abraham. He treated the Karaites as members of the family estranged ; he sought not
their annihilation but their restoration to the

family hearth. Weiss suggests that Maimonides' ruling passion for simplifying the Rabbinical exposition of Judaism was due to his desire to win the Karaites back to their allegiance. He eliminated the Karaite customs that had crept into Rabbanite life, and resisted the authority and influence of the followers of Anan. But he won by love more than by hostility, and thus his triumph over Karaism in Egypt was what Ben Sira calls the most laudable of victories, for he destroyed his foes by converting them into friends.

To return to an earlier period, to the time of Maimonides' arrival in Cairo. He himself describes the condition of the community in a document dated 1167.[18] "In times gone by, when storms threatened us, we wandered from place to place ; but by the mercy of God we have now been enabled to find a resting-place in this city. On our arrival we noticed to our great dismay that the learned were disunited ; that none of them turned his attention to what was going on in the congregation. We therefore felt it our duty to undertake the task of guiding the holy flock, of reconciling the hearts of the fathers to their children, and of correcting their corrupt ways. The mischief is great, but we may succeed in effecting a cure, and in accordance with the words of the prophet :

'I will seek the lost one, and that which has been cast out I will bring back, and the broken one I will heal.'" Practical effect was given to Maimonides' zeal, and henceforward he never allowed his interest in wider concerns to preclude a very real devotion to local affairs. One might rather say that his presence in Cairo transfigured local affairs into matters of world-wide moment. His livelihood was still derived from the business in precious stones, in which his brother David was the more active partner.[19] Nothing in all that Maimonides wrote exceeds in vehemence his denunciation of those who lived by their learning, and who served the Synagogue or the school for gain.[20] He returns to the subject again and again; he would have colleges without revenues and teachers without salaries. His ideal was that of the old Mishnaic sages; the scholar, like the layman, must live from the toil of his hands. The change in Jewish life against which Maimonides protested was not wide-spread till the fourteenth century. Yet the change was inevitable. The demands of the community on its official heads became ever more onerous; the incompatibility between the Rabbinic office and trade was daily more keenly felt. Besides, the practice of medicine required little scientific training

in the twelfth century, and Rabbis (like
Maimonides himself a little later in his life)
could double the parts of the healer of body
and soul. But the great medieval universities
established a higher standard of qualification,
and the medical profession soon required an
undivided devotion. Theology, too, became
more absorbent of a man's whole mind and
heart, and the Rabbinical function demanded
all that a man had to give. Still it is a
pleasing thing to contemplate the Rabbi of
Cairo, like the Sage of Amsterdam, pursuing
his intellectual career under the influence of
utterly unsordid motives.

Soon after his arrival in Egypt, Maimon
died. This was not the only sorrow that
now visited our hero. A spirit less resolute
than his must have been broken by the
succession of misfortunes which befell him.
"Physical sufferings threw him on a bed
of sickness; heavy losses diminished his
fortune; informers appeared against him,
and brought him to the brink of death."
We here have the echo of incidents in
Fez, and it is certain from Maimonides' own
testimony that at a later period he stood in
serious danger from the injurious charges of
informers. The final blow fell when his
brother David perished in the Indian Ocean,
and with him was lost not only their own

capital, but also the money placed with the
brothers by other traders. The loss of his
brother affected him sharply and enduringly.
He did not recover from the blow for many
years, and his letter to his friend Japhet,
written long after the catastrophe, bears
touching witness to the close sympathy that
had united the brothers.[21] " It is the heaviest
evil that has befallen me. His little daughter
and his widow were left with me. For a full
year I lay on my couch, stricken with fever
and despair. Many years have now gone
over me, yet still I mourn, for there is no
consolation possible. He grew up on my
knees, he was my brother, my pupil ; he
went abroad to trade that I might remain
at home and continue my studies ; he was
well versed in Talmud and Bible, and an
accomplished grammarian. My one joy was
to see him. He has gone to his eternal
home, and has left me confounded in a
strange land. Whenever I come across his
handwriting or one of his books my heart
turns within me, and my grief re-awakes.
I should have died in my affliction but for
the Law, which is my delight, and but for
14.* philosophy, which makes me forget to moan."

After the death of his brother, Maimonides
abandoned commerce in favour of medicine
as a means of earning his livelihood. His

fame as a physician belongs to a later period
in his career. At first he was an unknown
man, and his practice was not extensive.
Alkifti informs us that he gave public lectures on philosophical subjects, but neither
his medical nor his tutorial pursuits kept
him from occupying his mind with the completion of the work which he had begun
in Spain in his twenty-third year, and had
spasmodically continued by land and sea during the vicissitudes of his troubled life.

The year 1168 witnessed the completion
of the *Siraj* (Hebrew, *Maor*) or " Light," as
the " Commentary on the Mishnah " was
named. The fate which marked its incep-
tion accompanied the work to its close.
Begun amid danger, the *Siraj* was finished
in turmoil. For in 1168 Fostat, his new
home, was the scene of the final conflict in
the struggle between Almaric and Shirkuh
for the mastery of Egypt. The King of
Jerusalem had alienated the Egyptians by a
wholesale massacre at Bilbeys, and the dila-
toriness of the Christian advance gave the
people of Cairo an opportunity to make
heroic preparations. " The old city of Fostat, for three hundred years the metropolis of
Egypt and still a densely populated suburb of
Cairo, was by Shawar's orders set on fire,
that it might not give shelter to the Franks.

Twenty thousand naphtha barrels and ten
thousand torches were lighted. The fire
lasted fifty-four days, and its traces may still
be found in the wilderness of sand-heaps
stretching over miles of buried rubbish on
the south side of Cairo. The population re-
occupied the burnt city to some extent for a
century, and its final abandonment and demolition dates from the reign of Beybars." [22]
Cairo, despite this destruction of its oldest
suburb, was soon to be made greater and
nobler than ever. The Fatimids had relied
for security on their fortified palace in the
plain. With his military genius Saladin saw
that the extension of the city to the north-east
was dangerous. He chose the most western
spur of Mount Mukattam for a new citadel, the famous "Castle of the Mountain,"
the view from which, over Nile and desert,
dotted with Arab mosques and Pharonic
pyramids, still affords one of the most magnificent prospects in the world. From the
citadel may still be seen traces of the new
pleasure-gardens with which Saladin beauti-
fied the city. Fostat itself, which lay south-
west of the citadel and close to the Nile, was
to be included within Saladin's fortifications.
This part of the plan was abandoned, and now
very little is left of the old site. But the Synagogue, standing near soil which, though close

to the ancient Fostat, has been recovered
from the river since Maimonides' day, has
recently brought the place to fame once
more.   For there is situate the *Geniza* or
buried treasury from which so many lost
gems of Hebrew literature have been recovered.   The so-called Maimonides Synagogue is not in Fostat at all, and has
no authentic connection with Maimonides.
The Geniza is Cairo's most famous Jewish
relic of the medieval ages, but England has
spoiled the Egyptians, and Cambridge rather
than Fostat now holds a large part of the
Jewish treasures from the banks of the Nile.

CHAPTER V

The "Siraj"—Commentary on the Mishnah

1168

THE fame of the *Siraj* has been eclipsed by
the maturer works of its author, yet it presents in germ the main ideas which he afterwards developed. Again, the Commentary
of Maimonides has not been as popular an
aid to the study of the Mishnah as the useful
but more commonplace work of a later ex-
positor, Obadiah of Bertinoro. So high a
modern authority as Strack pronounces the
commentary of Maimonides indispensable for
the study of the Mishnah, and at the present
time the importance of the *Siraj* is fully
recognised. Maimonides wrote his *Siraj* in
Arabic, and among the contemporaries of
the author some actually preferred the
Siraj to the great Code (the *Mishneh-*

Torah) for the very reason that the former
was composed in Arabic, the vernacular
spoken by a large section of Jews. A
good deal of the *Siraj* was also translated
into Hebrew during the lifetime of Maimonides, and the desire for a complete
Hebrew version was widely felt.[23] The *Siraj*
has had a great and deserved influence on
Jewish theology. " Clearness, method, sym-
metry," are the qualities which Graetz detects
in the *Siraj*. " The construction of the
Talmud," writes the same historian, " seems
opposed to an orderly arrangement." But
Maimonides demonstrated that this absence
of system is a superficial defect. The Talmud readily lends itself to codification, given
the qualifications which Maimonides pre-
eminently possessed, an easy mastery over the
subject-matter, and a sound conception of
logical method. In these respects Maimonides stands supreme. As Simeon Duran said
of him : " His like has not existed for bringing things close to men's understanding." [24]
He had a profound reverence for the Talmud, and applied to the Rabbinical tradition
the Scriptural text, " Thou shalt not add to
it nor take away from it." But he maintained that not everything enshrined in the
Rabbinical literature deserves to be taken
literally or to be regarded as " traditional."

Sometimes he dissents from the Talmudical explanations of the Mishnah, even, according to Weiss, in cases where the *halachah* or practical law is affected.[25]   His respect for authority was tempered by a belief in his own powers, especially when dealing with the decisions and explanations of his nearer predecessors. Again, we find Maimonides attaching great importance to the Agadic elements in the Rabbinical literature as sources of ethical and philosophical truth.   The process of reading an esoteric meaning into these elements as well as into certain features of Scripture was carried out more fully in the " Guide of the Perplexed," the last great work of our author. But the idea had already taken firm hold of Maimonides.   " In the (allegorical) discourses of the Talmud," he writes, in his *Siraj*, " lies much profound teaching.   Let a man get a thorough intellectual insight into these discourses, let him realise the hidden store of true good therein contained and beyond which there is nothing more excellent, then will be revealed to him matters of divine truth, and much that the philosophers have spent their lives in searching for.   But the sages hid these things and desired not to reveal them openly, so that the mind of the student might be sharpened, and so that these matters might remain a secret from those whose in-

tellect was inadequate to receive truth in its
purity." Maimonides, with an analysis which
applies also to our own day, discriminates [26]
between three classes of those who study the
words of "our sages of blessed memory."
The first class take everything in its literal
sense, and eulogise the sages for the very
things which bring them into obloquy ; the
second class, again accepting everything as
literal, pour ridicule on the Rabbis ; the
third class ("so small," says Maimonides,
"that we can scarcely term them a class ")
hold the Rabbinical utterances in the deepest
reverence, but understand that there is an
exoteric and esoteric, an open and a hidden
sense in the words of the Rabbis. Thus
Maimonides was already preparing himself
to take the lead in medieval scholasticism
and to found a philosophy of religion on a
basis, at first unconsciously, yet in the end
essentially, constructed on a syncretism between Greek metaphysics and Hebrew
revelation.

Besides gathering into a short compass the
quintessence of the Talmud, "his originality,"
says Dr. Friedländer,[27] " is conspicuous in the
Introduction, and in the treatment of general
principles, which in some instances precedes
the exposition of an entire section or chapter,
in others that of a single rule. The com-

mentator is generally concise, except when
occasion is afforded to treat of ethical and
theological principles, or of a scientific subject, such as weights and measures, or mathematical and astronomical problems. Although
exhortations to virtue and warnings against
vice are found in all parts of his work, they
are especially abundant in the Commentary
on Aboth, which is prefaced by a separate
psychological treatise, called 'The Eight
Chapters.' The dictum, 'He who speaketh
much commits a sin,' elicited a lesson on the
economy of speech ; the explanation of *olam
ha-ba* [the future world] in the treatise Sanhedrin, led him to discuss the principles of
faith, and to lay down the Thirteen Articles
of the Jewish Creed." These excursuses
though incidental were not *obiter dicta*. The
author insists again and again that they are
the result of wide research and long and careful thought. He demands of his readers the
same diligence in perusal that the author had
expended in composition. The general introduction to *Tohoroth* is pronounced by Frankel
a masterpiece.

It is necessary to linger a little over two of
the excursuses alluded to in the foregoing excellent summary. Of the psychological excur-
sus, known as "The Eight Chapters," [28] it
may be said that it is the most remarkable

instance in medieval ethical literature of a syncretism between Hebraism and Hellenism. It
is thoroughly Jewish in thought ; it is Hellenic
in form. It is a treatise on the health and
sickness of the soul ; on the means by which
the sickness may be transformed into health.
" Ethics are the medicine of the soul," the
Greek scientific view, and " All thine actions
shall be to the glory of God," the ancient
Mishnaic conception, are the texts on which
Maimonides discourses. It is in the fourth
of " The Eight Chapters " that we come across
the famous attempt of Maimonides to apply
to Jewish ethics the Aristotelian doctrine of
the *Mean*. As far back as Hesiod, $\mu\acute{\epsilon}\tau\rho\iota\alpha$ $\acute{\epsilon}\rho\gamma\alpha$
are the object of praise, and over the temple
of Delphi was inscribed the motto $M\eta\delta\grave{\epsilon}\nu$
$\acute{\alpha}\gamma\alpha\nu$. To the Greek the moral sense, like
the musical ear, is satisfied by harmony. If
virtue be harmony, beauty in action, then
Aristotle's $M\epsilon\sigma\acute{o}\tau\eta\varsigma$ (*Mean*) perfectly expresses
the principle of virtue. Excess and deficiency
lie at the two extremes, and each is evil ; between them runs the Mean, which is the Good.
Virtuous action is a balance, the virtuous soul
is symmetrical, graceful. Thus the principle
of Ethics is the same as that of Art, though, as
Aristotle puts it, " Moral Virtue is finer than
the finest Art." " That beauty constituted
virtue," writes Grant,[29] " was an eminently

Greek idea. If we run through Aristotle's list of virtues, we find them all embodying this idea. The law of the $M\epsilon\sigma\acute{o}\tau\eta\varsigma$, as exhibited in bravery, temperance, liberality, and magnanimity, constitutes a noble, free, and brilliant type of manhood. Extend it also, as Aristotle does, to certain qualifications of temper, speech, and manners, and you have before you the portrait of the graceful Grecian gentleman." The doctrine of the Mean, however, fails to explain the relation of the will to morals. It offers no explanation of the " impulse to truth—the duty of not deceiving." Nor can it be said that the peculiarly Hebraic virtues, unrecognised as such by Hellenism—humility, charity, forgiveness of injuries—are explicable by the theory of the Mean. In the Jewish " Wisdom of Solomon " the idea of beauty is applied to wisdom, but no Jewish moralist could be content with beauty as a full theory of ethics. If, continues Grant, we ask whether these peculiarly Hebraic (Grant calls them Christian) qualities are mean states, " we find that they are all beautiful ; and, in so far as that, they all exhibit a certain grace and balance of the human feelings. There is a point at which each might be overstepped : humility must not be grovelling, nor charity weak ; and forgiveness must at times give place

to indignation. But there seems in them
something which is also their chief characteristic, and which is beyond and different
from this quality of the Mean. Perhaps this
might be expressed in all of them as 'self-
abnegation.' Now here we get a different
point of view from which to regard the virtues,
and that is the relation of Self, of the individual Will, of the moral Subject to the objective in the sphere of action. This point of
view Aristotle's principle does not touch.
Μεσότης expresses the objective law of
beauty in action, and as correlative with it,
the critical moral faculty in our minds, but
the law of right in action as something
binding on the moral subject it leaves unexpressed. . . . Μεσότης expresses the beauty
of good acts, but leaves something in the
goodness of them unexpressed." This criticism, however, does not apply to Maimonides,
however effective it be against Aristotle.
Maimonides, it is true, describes all virtues as
mean states, but his list of virtues is derived
not from his metaphysics but from Scripture.
Scripture is the ultimate source of well-doing ;
it is to the Scriptural virtues that Maimonides
applies the doctrine of the Μεσότης, not as
explaining their intent but as defining and
limiting their content. Critics of Aristotle
are inclined to forget that the doctrine of the

59

Mean is at all events an instrument for the analysis of moral concepts and that such an *analysis* has real ethical value. It cannot be doubted that to Judaism, at all events, this analysis was salutary and needful. In Maimonides' hands the law of the Mean becomes a valuable ethical corrective ; he uses it in behalf of a sane piety, and urges the avoidance of those excesses of pietism which tend to convert virtue into a disease. It is no pallid, colourless character that Maimonides conceives as the ideal. His is a strenuous standard ; but it is righteousness, not over-righteousness that he preaches. Yet disease may need poison to remedy it. So, he explains, the cure of a spiritual deficiency may consist in a spiritual excess, and for a great moral reformation it may be imperative to pass from extreme evil to extreme good, so that finally the Mean may be recovered and firmly held. The Greek law of beauty would require, as its correlative, a law of necessary deformity. Morality is not so much harmony as adjustment.[30]

"Every Israelite has a share in the world to come," runs a Mishnah in Tractate Sanhedrin. But who is an "Israelite," and what is the "life to come"? These questions suggested to Maimonides the desirability of examining current conceptions of immortality,

and forced upon him the duty of formulating
the ultimate doctrines, belief in which made
the Israelite. The essay in which Maimonides attempts to solve these problems is
unquestionably the most significant section
of the *Siraj*.[31]   He opens with the lament that
many take a material view of eternal bliss,
conceiving it as a Garden of Eden, where
flow rivers of wine and spiced oils ; and men,
free from toil, inhabit houses built of precious
stones, and recline on silken couches.   Hell
to them is equally materialised, as a place of
burning fires and bodily torments.   Others,
again, attach their hopes of bliss to the conception of an approaching Messianic Age, in
which men will be as kings, living eternally,
gigantic in stature, provided by a bountiful
earth with garments ready woven and meats
ready baked.   A third class rest their hopes
on the Resurrection, believing that a man
will be in a happy state if, after his death, he
live again with his dear ones and household,
eating and drinking, but never again dying.
Yet others hold that the good derived from
obedience to the divine law consists in earthly
happiness, and that earthly misery and " captivity " result from disobedience.   A fifth
class, a very numerous section, combine all
these ideals, holding as their ideal that Messiah
will come, and will quicken the dead ; that

they will enter the Garden of Eden, and
eat there and drink, healthy throughout eternity. All of these base their views, in part
successfully, on Scripture and Tradition, but
they succeed by interpreting literally texts
that need to be explained as figures. The
real marvel and mystery, the whole conception of a future world, they do not attempt
to examine. They rather ask, " How will
the dead arise ?—naked or clothed ? attired in
the embroidered shrouds in which they were
interred, or dressed in simple garments to
cover their flesh ? " As to the coming of the
Messiah, they are concerned with such questions as, " Will all men, rich and poor, be equal
then ? Or will one be strong and another
weak ? " Now a wise teacher attracts the
child by nuts, and figs, and honey ; for the
child cannot appreciate the real purpose of
his studies. As the pupil grows older, the
reward must change, and the nuts having
palled, the teacher must charm with fine
shoes and dainty apparel. Later he will offer
more substantial bribes, such as money ; later
still he will say, Study to become a *dayan*, to
win men's respect, that the people may rise
before thee as they do before such and such
a one. But can a man of character and
intellect be satisfied with this ? Is the end of
wisdom to be found except in wisdom itself ?

Shall man learn except to win truth, or obey
the Law for any motive except obedience?
Man must study the Law simply to know it,
seeking truth for truth's own sake, and know-
ing in order to perform. It is unlawful to
say, I will follow the good to win reward,
and eschew the evil to escape punishment.
Maimonides is very forcible in maintaining
this view, and cites with affectionate approval
the saying of "that perfect man, who reached
the truth of things," Antigonus of Socho,
whose utterance has ever since been the keynote of the higher Judaism : " Be not like
servants who minister to their master upon
the condition of receiving a reward ; but be
like servants who minister to their master
without the condition of receiving a reward."
Maimonides follows this up by several apt
quotations in which Rabbinical sages inculcated "service from motives of love towards
God," especially the famous comment of
R. Eleazar on the text, "In His commandments he delights exceedingly," " In His commandments, not in the rewards for them,
he delights," and the equally famous saying in the Sifri, "All that you do must be
done for pure love of the Lord." What
then of the offers of reward and threats of
punishment ?

Maimonides answers by the theory which

he subsequently developed in explanation of
the Sacrifices. A concession was necessary to
the average man, who is incapable of such
pure devotion, but needs a specific stimulus,
just as the schoolboy does from his teacher ;
but the concession was a means to an end,
the end being the attainment of such a spiritual exaltation in which the love of good will
be the sole stimulus to good, and the ideal
will be realised in a perfect knowledge of the
divine truth. Let men, said the Rabbi, serve
God at first for reward ; they will end by
serving Him without any such motive. Thus
the concession is educational. But Maimonides carries the argument farther. The
material rewards prescribed in Scripture were
aids to virtue rather than payment for it.
" When a man is sick, hungry, thirsty, or at
war, he cannot obey the ordinances of God.
The object of reward for obedience is not
that the land shall be fat, and men live long
and healthily, but that these blessings shall help
them to perform the law, while the penalties
of disobedience are penalties only in this that
man by his very sin is rendered incapable of
serving God. "If" (Maimonides puts this
into God's mouth) " thou performest part
of a single ordinance from love and desire,
I will help thee to perform all ordinances, and
will ward off all obstructive ill ; but if thou

leavest one thing undone from motives of
contempt, I will bring on thee consequences
which will prevent thee from obeying the
whole law." Now it may be that Paradise
will give to the righteous all that men dream
of delight, and more ; and Gehenna may be
a fiery torture for the wicked. The days of
the Messiah will fulfil all that the prophets
have prophesied, and Israel will regain the
sovereignty and return to their land. But
our hope in the Messiah is not made up of
dreams of wealth or hopes of Eden—a
dream of bliss to spur us to righteousness.
Eternal bliss consists in perfect spiritual
communion with God. " He who desires
to serve God from love must not serve to
win the future world, but he does the right
and eschews the wrong because he is man,
and owes it to his manhood to perfect
himself ; and this effort brings him to the
type of perfect man, whose soul shall live in
that state which befits it, viz., in the world
to come."

Maimonides follows up this striking pro-
nouncement by a formulation of the thirteen
fundamental principles of Judaism : (1) Belief
in the existence of a Creator ; (2) Belief in
His Unity ; (3) Belief in His Incorporeality ;
(4) Belief in His Eternity ; (5) Belief that all
worship and adoration are due to Him alone ;

(6) Belief in Prophecy ; (7) Belief that Moses
was the greatest of all Prophets ; (8) Belief
in the Revelation of the Law to Moses at
Sinai ; (9) Belief in the Immutability of the
Law ; (10) Belief that God knows the acts
of men ; (11) Belief in Reward and Punishment ; (12) Belief in the Coming of the
Messiah ; and (13) Belief in the Resurrection
of the Dead. "The great majority of
Jews," says Prof. Schechter,[32] "accepted the
Thirteen Articles without further question.
Maimonides must indeed have filled up a
great gap in Jewish theology, a gap, moreover, the existence of which was very
generally perceived. A century had hardly
elapsed before the Thirteen Articles had
become a theme for the poets of the
Synagogue. And almost every country
where Jews lived can show a poem or a
prayer founded on these Articles. R. Jacob
Molin (1420) of Germany speaks of metrical
and rhymed songs in the German language,
the burden of which was the Thirteen
Articles, and which were read by the common
people with great devotion. The numerous
commentaries and homilies written on the
same topic would form a small library in
themselves." Though, however, the Thirteen
Articles have been received into the Synagogue ritual in two separate forms,[33] they

have not been accepted without criticism.
Maimonides apparently considered the Articles
as dogmatic tests, and in a very peculiar
sense. "If a man believes these Articles,"
he writes, "he is included in the category
of Israelite, and it is a duty to love him.
Should he be led to commit transgressions
by the urgency of his lust and the dominance
of his lower nature, he will be punished for
his offences, but he has a share in the future
world. If, however, he rejects any of these
Articles, he has withdrawn himself from the
category of Israelite; he has denied the
principles of Judaism, he is a heretic and
unbeliever, a lopper of the tree, and it is
a duty to hate him and destroy him."
Maimonides was the first Rabbanite Jew
to attempt such a formulation of the creed
of Judaism, and he did it at a period when
the Jews had long ceased to possess any
central authority qualified to promulgate
dogmatic tests. Neither Papacy nor Church
Council was available, but Maimonides was
not free from the intolerance which sometimes presided over both. Chasdai ibn
Crescas in his "Light of God" (1405)
contended that "Maimonides confounded
dogmas or *fundamental beliefs* of Judaism,
without which Judaism is inconceivable,
with beliefs or *doctrines* which Judaism in-

67

culcates, but the denial of which, though involving a strong heresy, does not make Judaism impossible." But much of the criticism of Chasdai is really irrelevant. Maimonides himself was far more tolerant in spirit than he represents himself. When Chasdai objects that Reward and Punishment, Immortality and Resurrection, "must not be considered as the basis of Judaism, since the highest ideal of religion is to serve God without any hope of reward," he is only repeating the remarks of Maimonides cited above. Again, Chasdai points out that the Immutability of the Law is not a dogma, for "the perfection of the Torah could only be in accordance with the intelligence of those for whom it was meant; but as soon as the recipients of the Torah have advanced to a higher state of perfection, the Torah must also be altered to suit their advanced intelligence." Maimonides, as we shall see, practically held the same view, for he claimed the right so to *explain* certain words of Scripture as to convert them into a new Scripture. Hence, though at the first blush it would seem that Maimonides set up rigid dogmatic tests to be applied with intolerant severity, yet in effect he placed no heavy trammels on the Jewish intellect and conscience. He did a real service to Judaism by re-establishing *belief* as the basis of *conduct*, and his words, "inlaid with pearls," made the spiritual conception of the divine nature and the divine law predominant for all time in Jewish theology. 20.*

CHAPTER VI

The Change of Dynasty

In March 1169 the Fatimid Khalif chose
Saladin as the least dangerous of all the
Syrian captains, and invested him with the
mantle of Vizir. Saladin now threw off his
old diffidence and vacillation ; the real man
stood revealed, to the surprise of friend and
foe. "When God gave me the land of
Egypt," said Saladin, "I was sure that he
meant Palestine for me also." Thus he
devoted himself to the Holy War, and vowed
himself the champion of Islam. Saladin's
position was for some years a difficult one.
He was the Vizir of the heretical (Shiite)
Khalif of Egypt, and the military representative of the orthodox (Sunnite) ruler of
Damascus. Thus Saladin's policy was to
avoid offending the religious susceptibilities
of the masses in Egypt, or arousing the
suspicions of his master Nureddin. The
struggle with the black Sudanese partisans

70

of the Fatimids was an obstinate contest, for these kept Egypt in a state of unsettlement for six years. Saladin, however, made short work of the Sudanese in the capital, and Cairo was freed from them in 1169. More formidable was the attack of the Crusaders, who, like Saladin, perceived that Egypt was the key to Palestine. But Amalric's attempt on Damietta was frustrated, though his machina or fighting tower rose seven stories high. In 1170 Saladin assumed the offensive, and making a raid on Gaza initiated the "series of attacks which continued until his treaty with Richard of England, twenty-two years later." [34]

These successes so firmly established Saladin's authority that Sunnites and Shiites alike accepted him as their champion. In 1171 Saladin took the bold step of deposing El-Adid, the last of the Fatimids, who lay dying at the moment and was not informed of his fall. Of the priceless treasures which he discovered in the abode of El-Adid Saladin retained nothing for his personal use ; he did not even take up his residence in the famous twin palaces of Cairo. Nureddin could not but feel alarmed at the growing power of his Egyptian lieutenant, and it needed all Ayyub's sagacity and tact to lull the suspicions entertained by the King of Syria against Ayyub's son. More than once Nureddin seriously thought of attacking Saladin, but his death in 1174 occurred before he had given effect to any such resolve. From 1174 till his death in 1193 Saladin's supremacy was unquestioned.

During the intervening years Saladin's firm hand preserved Cairo from disorder after the bloody fight with the blacks in the very courtyards of the palace. But until Nureddin's death Saladin was never free from a sense of insecurity. Thus he was always looking abroad for an asylum to which to flee should he be driven from Egypt by the lord of Syria. Among the various spots on which his eyes rested was one which now enters more closely into the career of Maimonides. Yemen, famed in ancient times as Arabia Felix, bounded on the west by the Red Sea, had filled an important place in the world's commerce from the reign of Solomon to the days of Cyrus. Romance added its charms to the land, and its Queen of Sheba still lives in history and myth. Later on the cupidity of Rome led to the expedition of Gallus in the Augustan age. Then for some centuries the country was the scene of a struggle for supremacy between Judaism and Christianity. Islam, seeing that Mecca was situate on the northern border of

72

Yemen, stepped in and snatched the prize from its older rivals. Saladin, until he sent his elder brother Turin Shah to Yemen in 1174, had but a weak hold there. The power was locally in the hands of a Shiite Mahdi, who like the Unitarians in Morocco associated their purer monotheism with a fanatical hostility towards every other creed but their own. Where Saladin really ruled, justice was enjoyed by all his subjects. In Cairo the Jews were prosperous, influential, and self-governed. But in Yemen persecution and not Saladin held sway. The old experience of Fez repeated itself. Offered the alternative between Islam and punishment, many became Moslems, at first outwardly, but they soon exchanged appearance for reality. It was even argued by a Moslem, formerly a Jew, that Mohammed was alluded to in the Bible, and the old argument was revived that Islam had superseded Judaism. "A Mahdi in Islam," says Mr. L. M. Simmons, "was often accompanied by a Messiah in Judaism." "To add to the dangers of the moment," writes Graetz, "there appeared a Jewish enthusiast in Yemen who proclaimed himself to be the forerunner of the Messiah, endeavoured to instil in the Jews the belief that their affliction was the harbinger of the speedy approach of the Messianic empire, and

73

bade them hold themselves in readiness for that event and divide their property with the poor. This enthusiasm, to which many clung as drowning men to a straw, threatened to bring the direst misfortunes on the heads of the Yemenite Jews. The pious abandoned themselves to despair in the contemplation of these proceedings, and altogether lost their heads." The pseudo-Messiah here alluded to was not David Alroy, though the two impostors were contemporaries.

One of the best representatives of the Yemenites, Jacob of Fayum, appealed to Maimonides in this crisis. In response he despatched his celebrated " Letter to the South " (*Iggereth Teman*), also known as the " Gate of Hope " (*Petach Tikvah*).[35] It was written in Arabic, but there are three distinct Hebrew translations of it. It was indeed a message of hope. Persecution, he argued, was in one sense a tribute to the presence of God in the camp of Israel. " Nations envy us our possession of the Law. They contend not with us but with God." Israel had been assailed in three forms : by the sword of Nebuchadnezzar and Titus; by the charm of Hellenism ; by Christianity and Islam in the mask of new revelations. This last was the subtlest attack, for the Sinaitic revelation was declared true, but

superseded. Maimonides now warned the
Yemenites against exchanging a living body
of flesh and blood for a beautiful inert statue,
which resembled the living model but lacked
heart and soul. Persecutions would never
cease, but, continued Maimonides, "*Israel
cannot be destroyed*." He argued, taking a
different line from his father Maimon, that
even if all the miracles of Jesus were proved,
he still would not be the Messiah. Jews
must judge not by the prophet, but by the
prophecy. "Judaism does not found its truth
upon its miracles, but upon the historical fact
of the revelation at Sinai." The whole
moral of the "Letter to the South" lay in
the words "Be strong." The Messiah will
come, but his advent must not be calculated.[36]
Certainly he will be as unlike the pretenders
in Ispahan and Yemen as it is possible to
conceive. Persecution is a trial of faith and
love. "Therefore, O our brethren of the
house of Israel, who are scattered to the
extremities of the earth, it is your duty to
strengthen each other, the great the small,
the few the many, and to raise your voice
in a faithfulness which shall never fail and
which shall make known publicly that God
is a Unity, unlike all other unities; that
Moses is his prophet, who spoke with him ;
that he is the Master of all the prophets

and the most perfect of all of them ; that
the Law from the first word to the last was
spoken by the Creator to Moses ; that nothing was to be abrogated in it, nothing to be
changed, nothing to be added thereto nor
taken therefrom, and that no other Law
than his will ever come from the Creator."
A modern theologian cannot but envy the
simplicity of this argument, and sigh at the
modern inapplicability of so easy a refutation
of men's doubts.   But we shall after all see
that though our hero ascribed to Moses all
the words of the Law, the interpretation of
those words was made to suit the metaphysics
of our Moses of the twelfth century.

The " Letter to the South " was not a
masterpiece of reasoning or exegesis, yet it
won a victory.   It was sent to Jacob Alfa-
yumi with the request that it be circulated
widely, and read publicly in all the congregations oi Yemen, before the wise and the
ignorant, before women and children.   But
the writer counselled caution, fearing further
disturbances should copies fall into wrong
hands.   There were in Islamic lands, as in
Christian, converts from Judaism who not
only sought to prove the truth of their new
faith from the sacred Scriptures of their old
religion, but kept a watchful eye on their
former brethren, and stood ready to act as

denunciators. Maimonides was conscious, too, that he was running serious risk by his intervention, but he did not allow such selfish apprehension to deter him. His intervention was completely successful. The Yemenite Jews were roused to enthusiasm, saner and more enduring than that produced by the local "Messiah." The latter had a genuine faith in himself, and solemnly challenged the king to decapitate him, asserting that he would still live. "The experiment was tried, but in this case faith produced no miracle." Maimonides did not restrict his service to words. He turned his growing influence at Cairo to account, and when in 1174 Saladin's brother assumed the reins of government in Yemen, the material condition of the Jews followed their spiritual condition on the road to better things. In the daily Glorification Prayer (*Kaddish*) the grateful Yemenites included a complimentary allusion to Maimonides,[37] thus showing him an honour usually reserved for the Prince of the Captivity in Bagdad on the day of his accession to office.

One of the curiosities of the middle ages is the rapidity with which news spread. The fame of Maimonides was soon in every mouth. Chief of the methods by which influence radiated was correspondence. The

"Letter to the South" was an epistle in
reply to a direct communication. Every
Rabbi was the recipient of a huge correspondence, which mostly assumed the shape
of questions on theoretical and practical
religion. Maimonides boasts that he never
failed to reply to any letter, except when he
was too ill to write.[38] He moreover tells us
that he always answered with his own hand,
and declined the use of a secretary lest he
be suspected of arrogance. This statement
chimes in well with the recent discoveries
in the Cairo *Geniza*, for many "Questions"
addressed to him have been found with his
autograph answer attached. His replies are
as clear as they are terse. We perceive in
them the author's invariable qualities. When
the point referred to him is halachic (a matter
of practical law), he gives his decision without
dialectics. When, however, the question
gives opportunity to lay down general principles of law or theology he freely avails himself of the chance. Many of his "Responsa"
that have been preserved to us elsewhere as
well as in the *Geniza* are full of interest.[39]
They belong in large part to a later period
of his life, when Saladin had left Egypt
(which he did in 1174) and Maimonides
was private physician to the Vizir Alfadhel.
By 1177 Maimonides appears to have been

recognised as the official head of the Cairo Jews. He established an ecclesiastical board with nine colleagues, and set himself to such diverse ends as to bring decorum into public worship and to eliminate Karaism without severity towards Karaites. From one of his "Responsa" we gather the interesting information that the education of girls was not neglected in Fostat.[40] In another he replies to an aged correspondent who styles himself ignorant, and laments his inability to read the Hebrew works of Maimonides. "Call not thyself ignorant, but my pupil and my friend, both thou and all who seek to cleave to the study of the Law. Abase not thyself, and do not despair of the attainment of perfection."[41] Maimonides' sympathy with human nature is revealed in these replies to an extent for which his formal treatises hardly prepared us. So with his humour and good sense. He was asked about a tallith (or scarf used at prayer) on which the worshipper had embroidered texts, to the disapproval of the local Rabbi. To the worshipper he said : " As thou servedst God in making it, so serve God in discarding it, and prevent dispute ; " while to the precisionist Rabbi he added : " A Rabbi should rule with a gentle hand, nor should he interfere where interference is unnecessary."

79

Maimonides

In another response he again urges harmony : "We hear too much of unions in Israel; let us hear more of union." He indignantly repudiated the suggestion that the ritual law should be made more stringent in the case of the ignorant, lest they "break down the fence." "Shall we establish a safeguard to a safeguard?" he sarcastically asked. "It is enough to rely on the traditional safeguards without troubling the community with further restrictions." When he had before him the case of an *aguna* (or wife whose husband had left her, and was probably dead), he said : "Our general principle must be to accept the *aguna's* testimony" (as to her husband's death) "without undue scrupulosity, for the judge that cross-examines her too rigidly does ill." The *aguna* needed all the Rabbi's sympathy in the middle ages. Again, the curious system of feeing "ten men of leisure" for the purpose of forming a "congregation" called from him the striking statement: "The intention of this institution" (alluded to in the Jerusalem Talmud) "was that there should be in every place ten men appointed to serve the public weal, and that should any communal or religious affair need their attention, they should leave their work and betake themselves to the synagogue. Therefore they said, 'Men at leisure *from their work,*' and they did not say, 'Idlers *without work*'; and in the Talmud reference was made to the attendance of these ten *at synagogue,* because the synagogue was the meeting-place for all engaged in philanthropy or in meeting sudden crises."

"A physician," he says in his *Siraj,* "should begin with simple treatment, trying to cure by diet before he administers drugs." In his "Responsa" he applies this principle to spiritual ills. He is sometimes soothing, sometimes severe and vehement. He applied the gentle as well as the severe cure to the Karaites, and his success (as has been mentioned above) lay not so much in humiliating them as in re-attaching them to Rabbinism. "He made of Israel again one people, and brought one to the other, so that they became one flesh," said a French eulogist of him. Nachmanides also attributes to Maimonides many such conversions, and the author of that remarkable book of travels, *Eben-Sappir* ("Sapphire-Stone"), informs us that the practical extinction of the Karaites in Arabic-speaking lands is due to the influence of Maimuni (to call Maimonides by another of his usual titles).[43] Reference has already been made to the attitude of Maimonides towards the Karaites. He tolerated no weakening of the Rabbinical laws of *tahara* (ritual purity), and in 1177 publicly denounced in Synagogue Karaite neglect in this respect. Women who followed the Karaite licence were deprived of their rights under the Kethuba (marriage contract).[44] But Maimonides did not allow this opposition to destroy his kindly feeling towards Karaites or others who differed from him in religious matters. He informed one of his correspondents that it was quite lawful to teach Christians the Law ; and to a convert to Judaism from Islam he wrote : "The Moslems are in no sense idolaters ; such a thing has long been cut off from their lips and their heart ; they maintain, as is fitting, the Unity of God." He even refused to call superstitions the stone-throwing at Mecca and the prostrations at prayer. "These things," he said, "have a pagan and superstitious origin, but they must not now be called superstitions, for their origin no longer dominates the meaning attached to these ceremonies." This is clearly the only safe view to take of ceremonial. Its religious worth depends almost as much on the spiritual significance attached to it as on its historical origin.

Perhaps Maimuni's most remarkable utterance is contained in that same "Responsum," in which he castigated a foolish Jewish scholar who had pained a convert from Islam by a reference to his origin. "When thy

teacher called thee a fool for denying that
Moslems are idolaters, he sinned grievously,
and it is fitting that he ask thy pardon, though
he be thy master. Then let him fast and
weep and pray; perhaps he will find forgiveness. Was he intoxicated that he forgot the
thirty-three passages in which the Law ad-
monishes concerning 'strangers'? Thus, even
if he had been in right and thou in error, it
was his duty to be gentle; how much more,
when thou hadst the truth and he erred!
And when he was seeking whether a Moslem
is an idolater, he should have been cautious
how he angered himself against a proselyte of
righteousness and put him to shame, for our
sages have said, 'He who gives way to his anger
shall be esteemed in thine eyes as an idolater.'
And how great is the duty which the Law
imposes on us with regard to proselytes.
Our parents we are commanded to honour
and fear; to the prophets we are ordered to
hearken. A man may honour and fear and
obey without loving. But in the case of
'strangers' we are bidden to love with the
whole force of our heart's affection. And
he called thee fool! Astounding! A man
who left father and mother, forsook his birthplace, his country and its power, and attached
himself to this lowly, despised, and enslaved
race; who recognised the truth and righteous-

ness of this people's Law, and cast the things of this world from his heart—shall such a one be called fool ? God forbid ! Not witless but wise has God called thy name, thou disciple of our father Abraham, who also left his father and his kindred and inclined God-wards. And He who blessed Abraham will bless thee, and will make thee worthy to behold all the consolations destined for Israel; and in all the good that God shall do unto us He will do good unto thee, for the Lord 26.* hath promised good unto Israel."

CHAPTER VII

The "Mishneh-Torah" or Religious Code

1180

THE most brilliant period in the Moslem rule over Egypt coincides with the twenty-four years of Saladin's domination (1169–1193).[45] But the glory came from without. Like his great rival, Richard I. of England, Saladin spent but a small portion of his reign in his capital. He passed but eight years in Cairo; the other sixteen were occupied in campaigns in Syria, Mesopotamia, and Palestine. It was, however, no detriment to Egypt that Saladin's policy was defensive and consolidating by the Nile, and aggressive only in Palestine. Cairo advanced far in spirit and intellect, while war was incessant in the other lands over which Saladin claimed and exercised authority. While Maimonides was making Fostat the

85

new centre of Judaism, Islam under Saladin also established its headquarters in the old capital of the Fatimids.

Saladin fortified Cairo with a citadel, but like the Rabbinical sage of old, he recognised that the real guardians of a city are not its soldiers but its scholars. The introduction into Cairo of the *Medresa* or Collegiate Mosque was the work of Saladin. The *Medresa*, with its regular courses of instruction, its comprehensive range of studies, its free popular lectures, was an innovation from Persia. Nureddin had imported the institution into Syria, Saladin carried it into Cairo and Alexandria. The Fatimid "Hall of Science" had to some extent forestalled the *Medresa*, but the Fatimids had devoted their energies solely to the mysticism of the Shia and to its speculative philosophy. When Saladin captured the treasures of the Fatimids, he handed over the noble library of 120,000 manuscripts to the Kadi Alfadhel. On his accession to power, Saladin not only retained the services of Alfadhel (who had been employed in the secretariat of the Fatimid khalif) but made him Vizir, and it says much for the characters of both, that Alfadhel retained his influence throughout Saladin's reign. Maimonides became one of the Vizir's physicians in or about 1185, and during the

last thirty years of Maimonides' life, Alfadhel
the Vizir was practically ruler of Egypt.
Alfadhel was worthy of his master, who
trusted him implicitly. Like many of the
statesmen of his day, Alfadhel was not a Turk
or a Persian, but a pure Lakmi Arab, born in
Ascalon. Notable among the notabilities at
Saladin's court, Alfadhel was " sovereign of the
pen," who " threaded discourse with pearls of
style." His devotion to culture, and especially to the promotion of it in Cairo, his
practical affection for the *Medresa*[46]—he
founded one himself—make him of great
importance to the career of Maimonides, who
received honours and encouragement from
the Vizir. Alfadhel, it is true, was often
absent in body from Cairo, but never in
spirit. " Bear me a message to the Nile,"
he wrote when engaged in a campaign in
Mesopotamia, " tell it that Euphrates can
never quench my thirst."

While Saladin was occupied in the conquest
of Syria, and was leading up to the capture of
Aleppo, Maimonides was winning possession
of a citadel, mastery over which conferred a
diadem more enduring and more honourable
than any that rested on Saladin's noble brow.
By the might of his genius, Maimonides
assailed with friendly hands the fastness
wherein lay enshrined the whole Jewish

lore. His victory is chronicled in the second
part of his great trilogy, in the *Mishneh-
Torah* ("Deuteronomy") or *Yad Hachazaka*
("Strong Hand"). This gigantic work, a
complete codification and digest of Biblical
and Rabbinical law and religion, occupied
him for ten years,[47] but when he completed it
in November 1180, the magnitude of the performance, with its fourteen books and one
thousand chapters, bore no relation to the
time which he had devoted to it. According
to an old tradition, the Mosaic enactments
numbered 613 (365 negative and 248 positive
commands). The Palestinian Rabbi Simlai,
of the third century, was the first to make
this statement explicit. In the eighth century,
Simon Kahira (author of the *Halachoth Gedo-
loth*) tabulated the 613 laws, and his list held
the field until the epoch of Maimonides.
The writers of the *Azharoth*, or didactic
hymns for recital at Pentecost, all adopted
Simon Kahira's enumeration. The very
popularity of this earlier list made it more
necessary for Maimonides to prepare one of
his own. To anticipate criticism of his
exclusions and inclusions, as well as to provide himself with a skeleton outline, he
compiled his *Sefer Hamitzvoth* (Book of the
Commandments), which though written in
Arabic has been thrice translated and is better

known in its Hebrew form.[48]   The list, afterwards prefixed by the author to the *Mishneh-
Torah*, displays, technical as it is, the best
qualities of Maimonides.   The Existence of
God, his Unity, the duty of loving him, of
fearing him, of serving him in prayer, of
cleaving to him, of swearing by his name,
of imitating his attributes, of sanctifying his
name : these are the first nine entries in
Maimonides' list of affirmative precepts.   He
builds up the ritual laws on these as a basis.
His grasp of general principles, his successful
search for generalities underlying details, his
power to bring to the front the spiritual side
of Judaism, of showing its expression in the
ritual side, these characteristics in a catalogue
of precepts reveal qualities which do not
fall short of genius.   To Maimonides the
ceremonial law was as sacred and as divine as
the ethical law ; but the spiritual, doctrinal
aspect not only came first, but justified and
transfigured the rest.

In the *Mishneh-Torah* the same spirit pre-
vails.   His Code is not only a unique monu-
ment of industrious compilation from Bible,
Talmud, and the whole Rabbinical literature.
The claim of the Code to esteem rests on its
manner as much as on its matter.   Graetz,
comparing the Talmud to a " Dædalian maze
in which one can hardly find his way even

with the thread of Ariadne," likens the
Mishneh-Torah to a " well-contrived ground-
plan, with wings, halls, apartments, chambers,
through which a stranger might pass without
a guide." There is some hyperbole in this
description of the intricacies of the Talmud,
but there is no exaggeration in its eulogy of
Maimonides. Judaism was in danger of losing
itself in detail. The *Mishneh-Torah* omitted
none of the details, whether significant or
trivial ; but on the one hand it systematised
them, and on the other it brought them into
relation with the fundamental postulates of
Judaism. Maimonides is never weary of
referring the student back to the starting-
point, to the nature and attributes of God,
to man's duty to imitate his Divine exemplar
and to act always with the love of God con-
sciously present as his sole motive and reward.
The marvel of the book is that this golden
thread of the spirit runs unbroken through
all the ritual details with which the Code
abounds, and thus in the *Mishneh-Torah* we
have the completest justification of the Jewish
conception of the relations between letter and
spirit, for the letter does not and cannot kill,
while the spirit gives it life. This was the
Talmudic spirit, and Maimonides in this
respect, as in many others, is a true son of
the tradition. In many respects, but not in

all. For his very systematisation of the
Talmud destroyed one of its best features.
Maimonides wrote his "Code" in the first instance for "his own benefit, to save him in his
advanced age the trouble and the necessity of
consulting the Talmud on every occasion." [49]
His plan, however, soon carried him beyond
his own immediate needs, and he ended by
compiling a complete digest, which in the
language of the Mishnah and *without discussion*
should offer a clear-cut decision of every
question touching the religious, ritual, moral,
and social duties of Jews. Had he succeeded
in winning for his Code unquestioned supremacy in Israel, tradition instead of retaining
its vitality must have become petrified, rigid
unto death. As it is, the effect of Maimonides' Code, and of the later Code (*Shulchan Aruch*) modelled on it, has not been
altogether beneficial from this point of view.
Hitherto, in all legal works, opinions had
been stated in the name of the original
authorities, decisions had been weighed in the
balance. Maimonides certainly discriminated
in theory between dicta meant literally and
figuratively, final decisions and individual
views ; between "traditions" and "deduc-
tions" ; between Rabbinical and Biblical laws
intended for all time and those restricted to
a particular occasion or locality. But in

practice he did not allow these distinctions
their due weight. Maimonides simply formed
his own opinion (mostly on the basis of sound
authority, it is true) and dogmatically announced it without reference to the nature
of his authority. Not only did he render
himself specially liable to attack when he fell
into error, but there can be no doubt that
Rabbi Abraham ben David of Posquières, in
his over-virulent criticism (*hassagoth*) on the
Code, placed his finger on a real and fundamental fault when he stoutly objected to the
dogmatism of the author.[50]

But Maimonides was bound to incur the
censure. His fault was the correlative of his
merits. To have reproduced the Talmudic
pilpul (dialectics) would have been to defeat
his main object. "If," he said, "I could
summarise the Talmud into one chapter, I
would not use two for the purpose." He
feared, too, that devotion to Talmudic
dialectics left no place and no leisure for
the pursuit of those other studies which he
held of equal importance. He wrote, moreover, for laymen as well as for experts, and
simplicity and system were the first requisites.
Alone of his three great works, the Code is
written not in Arabic but in Hebrew. He
chose a simple, lucid Hebrew akin to the
Mishnaic dialect; not the "prophetic style,"

for that would not harmonise with his
subject, and not the philosophical manner,
for that would be unintelligible to the
" general reader." He even refused to translate the *Mishneh-Torah* into Arabic.[51] He
did not employ the Aramaic idiom of the
Talmud because of its difficulty. It is too
much to assert, as some of his opponents
asserted, that he desired the supersession of
the Talmud ; but he certainly did expect,
though vainly, as the sequel proved, that his
compilation would be accepted as the quintessence of the Talmud, self-sufficient and
thus independent of its source.

Whether or not he was attempting the
impossible or the undesirable when he proposed to place the Law, defined and dogmatic, in the hands of all his brethren, his
conception of law was a great one. He
thought not only of the law of conduct.
Conduct was the spreading crown of
branches ; but reason, faith, spirituality
were the roots of the tree. The truth
won by Greece through philosophy was also
a truth belonging to Judaism. The principles of faith and love were the founts from
which it drew its life. The scriptural precepts were not arbitrary laws, but "judg-
ments of righteousness flowing from a deep
Well of Wisdom." " Is it just," he asked,

"to treat only of the branches and to neglect the roots of the tree;" to explore the river and neglect its springs? Thus the opening section of the Code is the famous *Sefer Hamada'* ("Book of Religious Philosophy"), famous intrinsically and for the fierce controversies to which it gave rise. His Code begins with these words: "The foundation of foundations and the pillar of all Wisdom is the recognition that an original Being exists, who called all creatures into existence; for the recognition of this thing is a positive command, and is the great principle on which all things hang." This strikes the keynote, and nobly the *Mishneh-Torah* proceeds on its way, codifying the "philosophical, the ethical, and ceremonial sides, and also the emotional side of Judaism as expressed in its Messianic ideals," until it culminates in its inspired close, speaking of the time when "the earth will be filled with the knowledge of God as the waters cover the sea." [52]

In a celebrated passage of the Code, at the end of the Hilchoth Melachim, he writes thus of the mission of Christianity and Islam: "The teachings of him of Nazareth (Jesus) and of the man of Ishmael (Mohammed), who arose after him, help to bring to perfection all mankind, so that they may serve God with one consent. For in that the

whole world is full of the words of the
Messiah, of the words of Holy Writ and the
Commandments—these words have spread to
the ends of the earth, even if many deny the
binding character of them at the present day.
And when the Messiah comes all will return 30.*
from their errors."

It is hard to say where Maimonides is at
his best in the *Mishneh-Torah* : as a careful
collator, " bringing together," to use his own
words, " things far off, scattered among the
hills " ; as a legal specialist, clearly formulating
a technical decision on a marriage law ; as an
astronomer compiling an original treatise on
the Calendar ; as an historian, prefixing to the
" Laws concerning Idolatry " a rapid yet
masterly sketch of the origin and development of nature-worship and pagan religion, and protesting against allowing any
taint of superstition to stain Judaism ; as the
moralist, writing of ethical theory and the
Law of the Mean, establishing principles of
charity of man to man, of Israelite to those
outside the pale ; as the ·intense believer,
urging the love of God with mystic thirst,
speaking of Atonement with a combination
of the divinest yearnings and consummate
good sense ; as the theologian, denying to
miracle its claim as a test of divine truth,
asserting man's free will ; as the meta-

95

physician, peering behind the veil of first
things. Part by part the work was issued
as it was completed, and little wonder that
those who obtained a portion longed for the
whole. There was no vanity in the titles
that he chose for it, *Mishneh-Torah* and
Mighty Hand, derived from the opening and
the close of the fifth book of Moses. It was
a repetition, or rather a renewal of the law
that Moses Maimonides presented to his
people. The sage of Cairo, the second
Moses, whom the Lord knew face to face,
had performed again in the same land by
the Nile " the signs and the wonders which
the Lord sent him to do in the land of
Egypt." He had once more revealed the
" mighty hand " with whose aid the first
Moses had " wrought in the sight of all
Israel." Verily, as the contemporaries of
Maimonides said of him, " From Moses unto
31.* Moses, there arose none like Moses."

CHAPTER VIII

Friends and Foes

THE fame of the "Code" spread rapidly throughout the Jewish world. Soon hundreds of professional scribes were industriously copying the work, to meet urgent demands from every land in which Jews resided, from Spain to India, from the sources of the Euphrates and the Tigris to Yemen, from Provence to England. Ardent enthusiasts made their copies with their own hands. If the admirers of Maimonides hoped that his *Mishneh Torah* would be canonised as an infallible guide, the event almost realised their dream. Specialists appreciated the performance on its legal and technical sides, and ordinary readers recognised with amazed delight that the sealed book of the Law had been opened to them at the touch of this mighty magician. "Bring near the Ephod," men said, when in their difficulties they made appeal, never in vain, to the Code of Mai-

97   G

monides.[53] The interest taken in this and
other works of the Cairo Rabbi by Christians and Moslems will be discussed in a later
chapter. As to his Jewish contemporaries,
the poets among them exalted him in their
songs, and incense was burned everywhere
at his shrines. As many thought and said,
none had done such service to the Law since
the days of Rabbi Judah the Prince, compiler
of the Mishnah.

It was not till after the death of Maimonides that the opposition to him assumed
serious proportions. Some premonitory notes
of the coming strife were sounded during his
lifetime, but the " Holy War " in Judaism did
not break out into fierce activity until the cause
of it lay in his honoured grave. Moreover,
the struggle turned rather on the author's third
important work than on his second, though
the first section of the *Mishneh Torah* shared
with the *Moreh* (" Guide of the Perplexed ")
the distinction of setting Judaism aflame.

The real friends of Maimonides were those
who seemed his foes. Had his infallibility
been accepted as a dogma, Judaism must have
sunk into a papacy governed by a dead pope.
The later form that the opposition took was
due to antipathy to his philosophy ; but the
earliest burst of disapproval was based on the
feeling that Maimonides must not be suffered

to become the autocrat of Jewish life. The author himself frankly admitted that his critics were sometimes right. Questions reached him from various sides. Often the doubts thrown on his accuracy were due to the sceptic's ignorance, or to the employment of other readings in the same texts. Sometimes, however, the error really lay with Maimonides ; in such cases he readily admitted his oversight, thanked his correspondents, and implored them to continue their minute examination of his work. "I had no other thought than to clear the way." No claim of infallibility emanates from *him*. "It is proper to examine my words closely and to inquire into my statements." [54] This type of criticism was thus welcomed by the author, and his rejoinders were gentle and conciliatory. But others of his critics were influenced by different motives. Some were animated by jealousy of the author. Some again feared that his simple, systematic reproduction of the Talmud would militate against the study of the Talmud in the original. This objection was not altogether unfounded, for in Yemen, where the Code of Maimonides received a peculiarly cordial welcome, the Talmud itself was thereafter almost completely neglected. In the Orient the " Code " again interfered seriously with "vested interests." Under Islam, the Jews in many places were self-governing ; not only under their *Resh Galutha* in Persia, their *Nasi* in Palestine, their *Nagid* in Egypt, but under less distinguished auspices in other parts of the Moslem world. In such communities the Talmud was chiefly used for practical law,[55] and the Code of Maimonides not only placed the layman at the same point of vantage as the Talmudist, but made the road to practical law so easy that the old lawyers were in danger of becoming superfluous. In Christian countries the Code was accepted in a more friendly spirit by the specialists of the old type. These did not regard Maimonides as their final court of appeal, but they cheerfully saw in him a new guide to set beside the old, a fresh aid to the study of the old lore with which their life was wrapped up. The chief exception to the latter class was R. Abraham ben David of Posquières. Of his opposition something has been already said. He was a wealthy man who had founded a college in his city, but his influence was due to his profound scholarship. He determined, in no spirit of personal hostility to Maimonides, to examine closely into every statement of the Code, and his notes (Hassagoth) are now usually printed in editions of Maimonides' Code, together with the counter-comments of R. Joseph Karo.

Friends and Foes

The object of the Rabad—as R. Abraham ben David is called, from the initials of his name—was to demonstrate that in many cases it was necessary to go behind Maimonides to his sources.[56] It is regrettable that the Rabad indulged in very violent and disrespectful language, but Maimonides himself was not free from this medieval habit of abusing men who happened to hold opinions differing from his own. Unfortunately the comments of the Rabad did not reach Maimonides, but after the death of the latter his accuracy was on the whole fully vindicated against his fiery opponent. Many of their differences arose from the fact that they had before them texts with various readings. Thus around the very Code itself there grew up a vast mass of that dialectical discussion from which the Code, in the author's intention, was to rescue Jewish law !   32.*

High on his official chair, mimicking the royal state of the Caliphate, Samuel ben Ali of Bagdad took an ignoble part in the opposition.[57] "Surrounded by his slaves armed with scourges, he would not acknowledge any one equal, much less superior to himself" (Graetz). By the claim that the College at Bagdad was the sole seat of Jewish authority, Samuel and his allies were attempting to crush the actualities of the present under the memories of the past. Secret slander was added to more honourable weapons of warfare. Yet the Gaonate had grounds enough for its dislike of Maimonides. Not only was he a formidable rival near the throne, but he had always set his face against the Persian luxury, and the revenues of the Bagdad College were to him anathema. Thus Maimonides at once endangered the official supremacy and challenged the moral integrity of the Gaonate. The Gaonate retaliated by depreciating the *Mishneh Torah*, and charging its author with inaccuracy and heresy. This opposition was no doubt fortified by a sense, instinctive rather than conscious in many, that Maimonides' conception of Talmudic Judaism was an innovation and a danger. That the hostility often assumed petty and malicious forms is no proof that the opposition was at bottom trivial or insincere. One may smile, as Maimonides himself did, at such critics as, nervous of their own repute, refused to cast their eye over the " Code " lest they be suspected of learning from it.

Maimonides acted under all this provocation with manly self-restraint. Even when Phineas ben Meshullam of Alexandria publicly preached against the book, Maimonides did not betray more than a momentary irritation. His letters breathe a spirit of large-mindedness and even aloofness, for though he was not cold as the proverbial philosopher, he was indifferent where smaller men would have been roused to indignation. " Honour bids me," he said, " to avoid fools, not to vanquish them. Better is it for me to spend my efforts in teaching those fitted and willing to learn than to waste myself in winning a victory over the unfit."[58]   To add to his causes of anxiety, he fell ill soon after the *Mishneh Torah* was completed. But neither the loud volume of general praise nor the slighter note of individual depreciation had power to move Maimonides. His joy and his consolation came from another source. One of the most delightful incidents in his whole life synchronised with this critical moment.

Among the *anusim*, or forced converts to Islam, in the Maghreb, was the lad Joseph Aknin. He had remained true to Judaism despite his superficial conformity to the dominant religion, and over and above his scientific and medical studies he had drunk deep at the well of the literature of Israel. On the one side an Arab of the Arabs, he wrote poems in the language of the Koran ; on the other a Jew of the Jews, he delighted in the Law all day. Joseph was about thirty years old when the fame of Maimonides reached him, and he hastened to leave his home and present himself before his master. On reaching Alexandria he wrote to Maimonides, explaining his ardent ambition to learn from the lips of the teacher whose books had already gained a hold over his spirit. Maimonides recognised in his correspondent a kindred mind, and welcomed Aknin with a cordiality that soon ripened into love. "If I had none but thee in the world, my world would be full," said Maimonides. Master poured out his heart to pupil, and when Aknin was forced to leave Cairo for Aleppo, the bond of affection between " father " and " son " was so firmly tied, that their friendship endured unto death. It was for Aknin that Maimonides wrote his third great work, the "Guide of the Perplexed." [59]

Aknin, who appears to have been a persistent traveller, was soon placed in a position to display his enthusiastic regard for his master. Arrived at Bagdad,[60] he found that the persistent efforts of Samuel ben Ali had succeeded in raising clouds of suspicion against Maimonides. Some of the latter's disciples, noting the tendency of Maimonides to spiritualise the conception of a future life, hastily concluded that they were justified in teaching, on his authority, that Judaism

denied the doctrine of a bodily resurrection.
When questioned on the point by his faithful
friends in Yemen, Maimonides explained
categorically that he did regard a belief in
the resurrection as a corner stone of Judaism.
This did not suffice for some of his critics,
who appealed to Samuel ben Ali for his
opinion. Delighted at the compliment and
at the opportunity of dealing his rival a blow,
Samuel ben Ali proceeded to collect passages
from the Agada and Midrash in which a
bodily resurrection is taught, and insisted that
all these utterances must be explained in their
strictly literal sense. To add to the piquancy
of his sting, the Bagdad Gaon quoted Moslem
philosophers on the same side, gleefully claiming that Jewish tradition and Arab metaphysics were at one against the heresies of
Maimonides. Joseph Aknin took up the
gauntlet, and for the moment diverted the
attacks of the Gaon on to himself. At last,
however, he could not endure the situation.
He despatched a full report to his master,
enclosed a copy of Samuel's treatise on the
resurrection, and entreated Maimonides to
reply to his assailants, and to retort on vice
the abuse which they had heaped upon
virtue. But Maimonides refused. His letter
to Aknin betrays much pathos, and over his
natural feeling of resentment, his good-sense

and magnanimity prevail. He tells Aknin that he foresaw what had occurred. He appreciates his disciple's youthful, hot-headed anger, and attributes his own indifference to physical weakness and to the calm produced by age. But his sorrow is unbounded that his friend should suffer on his behalf, suffer in his own person, and also because his soul was distressed at his master's obloquy. "My heart is pained in your pain, but you will please me better by actively propagating to men what is true than by setting yourself as my champion against the untrue. Teach, do not recriminate. Remember that you have injured this man, that his revenues are at stake. Shall such a man, being stricken, not cry? He concerns himself with what the multitude holds highest. Leave him to his trivialities, but what does he know of the soul and of philosophy? Remember he is old and occupies a position of dignity, and you are young and owe his age and position respect. You ask me as to your plan of opening a school in Bagdad in which you will teach the Law with my Code as the text-book. I have already sanctioned your proposal. Yet I fear two things. You will be constantly embroiled with these men. Or, if you assume the duty of teaching, you will neglect your own business affairs. I counsel you to take nothing from them. Better in my eyes is a single dirhem gained by you as a weaver, a tailor, or a carpenter, than a whole revenue enjoyed under the auspices of the head of the captivity."

Later on Maimonides himself was drawn into a controversy with Samuel over a point of law. "Custom," said Maimonides in reply to a correspondent from Bagdad, "is of weighty import. Yet the *custom* must not be confused with *law*. Error must never be allowed to persist. There is no distinction in this matter between prohibiting what is in truth lawful, or allowing what is in truth forbidden. Neither policy should be tolerated." This is a characteristic reply, for Maimonides, *à propos* of an insignificant question regarding the passage of rivers on Sabbath, lays down a general principle on the relation between custom and law. In the controversy that ensued with Samuel, Maimonides emerged triumphant, yet his respectful tone and humble manner failed to soften the Gaon's ill-will.

At this time Maimonides frequently refers to himself as an old and ailing man. Yet he was only fifty-one years of age, and had before him eighteen years of activity and happiness. He soon recovered from his despondency. In this very year his first and

only son (Abraham) was born to him. Maimonides had probably married in his youth,
but his wife must have died early.[61]   In Egypt
he married the sister of Abn-Almâli, one of
the royal secretaries.   The latter wedded the
sister of Maimonides, so that the two men
were doubly related.   It may well be that
much of our hero's despondency was due to
the fact that he was long childless.   Now,
however, his son Abraham, and Aknin, his
son in the spirit, cheered the prospect.   We
know little of his home-life, but what we do
know suffices to prove that as a husband and
father Maimonides was at once blessed and a
blessing.   He educated his son himself, cultivating his mind and soul ; nor did he withhold
from his own hearth that which he gave to the
world.

CHAPTER IX

The Holy War

1187–1192

"THE news of the fall of Jerusalem," writes Mr. Archer, "reached Europe about the end of October, 1187. It is hard at this distance of time to realise the measure of the disaster in the eyes of the Western world. It was not merely that the Holy City had fallen; that all the scenes of that Bible history, which constituted emphatically the literature of medieval Christendom, had passed into the hand of the infidel. It was all this and something more; the little kingdom of Jerusalem was the one outpost of the Latin Church and Latin culture in the East; it was the creation of those heroes of the First Crusade whose exploits had already become the theme of more than one romance; it lay on the verge of that mysterious East with all its wealth of gold and precious stones and merchandise, towards which the sword of the twelfth-century knight turned as instinctively as the prow of the English or Spanish adventurer four centuries later turned towards the West. . . . Thus Palestine inspired alike the imagination, the enterprise, and faith of Western Christendom." [62]

The response which Europe made to Saladin's challenge, the glories and horrors of the third Crusade, lie outside our present story. Egypt was scarcely affected by the struggle which for five years raged throughout the length and breadth of Palestine.[63] When Saladin vanquished the army of Guy of Lusignan at Hittin, near Tiberias, the conquest of Palestine and the capture of Jerusalem followed within a few months. Saladin, however, committed the fatal mistake of leaving Tyre in his enemies' hands, and this fortress by the sea became the rallying-point of the Franks. From Tyre marched, in 1189, the army which began the famous siege of Acre. Two days later Saladin besieged the besiegers, but after two years of heroism on both sides, the city surrendered to the Crusaders within five weeks of the arrival of Richard I. of England. At Arsuf Richard inflicted a serious defeat on Saladin, but neither the brilliant personal feats nor the military genius of the Lion-hearted King could counterbalance the dissensions which prevailed in the Christian camp. The noblest feature of the third Crusade was the chivalrous courtesy which marked the relations between Saladin and Richard, though the two men never met at a personal interview. In the end, Saladin's power was unshaken. The whole of Palestine, except a narrow strip of the coast from Jaffa to Tyre, remained in Saracen hands. It is remarkable with what fidelity Saladin was supported throughout the Holy War by every portion of his vast empire from Egypt to the Tigris. "Kurds, Turkmans, Syrians, Arabs and Egyptians mingled in his armies, and all were Moslems and his servants when he called upon them for an effort. Not a province had fallen away, only one youthful vassal rebelled for an instant, though trials and sufferings of the long campaigns had severely taxed the soldiers' endurance and faith in their leader." [64] Saladin had accomplished his ambition. He had re-united Islam. He had regained the Holy City, which, as he informed Richard on one occasion, was even more to the Moslem than to the Christian. "Jerusalem," replied Saladin to Richard's appeal, "is holy to us as well as to you, and more so, seeing it is the scene of our Prophet's journey, and the

place where our people must assemble at the
Last Day. Think not that we shall go back
therefrom, or that we can be compliant in
this matter." [65] And there the matter has
rested until our own day.

Egypt had served as a recruiting ground
for the army during the five exhausting years
of the Holy War. In all these campaigns,
actual warfare was confined to the summer.
Saladin's army did not go into winter quarters,
but the various contingents were sent home
to recover their vigour and to attend to their
personal concerns. A Moslem is never content to remain away from home for long,
and this policy of Saladin's helped to keep
his army content and spirited. Egypt
suffered less than might have been expected
from the constant drain of men.[66] For many
out of the levies returned for the winter, and
in Egypt the winter was the period for the
chief processes of agriculture. When the
Crusaders came within sight of Jerusalem,
though Richard himself averted his glance,
a Council of War decided on relinquishing
the scheme of attacking the Holy City in
favour of a march upon Cairo. If this
wearisome campaign of 250 miles over the
desert had been accomplished, the story of
Egypt might have been very different. But
as things turned out, the third Crusade left

Cairo as it found it, secure and faithful to
the Moslem cause.

Saladin's brother, el-Adil, with the co-
operation of the Kadi Alfadhel, of whom we
have already spoken, administered the affairs
of Egypt during and after the war. El-
Adil was the ablest and most "Western"
member of Saladin's family ; he was a skilful
general, a resolute fighter, a shrewd diplo-
matist, and absolutely loyal. Year by year
he led the Egyptian contingent to the annual
assemblage in Palestine. Not once did the
temptation to seize Egypt for himself rest in
his thought. His prowess and his personal
fascination made him a favourite with the
impetuous and lovable Richard. Cœur-de-
Lion even proposed a marriage between el-
Adil and his own sister Joan. El-Adil was
the intermediary between the two hosts in
the negotiations for the treaty of Ramleh,
which ended the war. During Maimonides'
last years, el-Adil was the recognised Sultan
of Egypt.

It may have been from el-Adil that Richard
heard of the fame of Maimonides as a medical
practitioner. The "King of the Franks in
Ascalon" sought his services as his physician,
but Maimonides declined the honour. He
was well content with his position under the
Vizir Alfadhel, and if he was acquainted with

the events which had occurred at Richard's coronation, he must have felt safer in Cairo than in London. Maimonides had made vast strides forward in medical proficiency and repute. As he wrote to Jonathan of Lunel: "Although from my boyhood the Torah (Law) was betrothed to me, and continues to hold my heart as the wife of my youth, in whose love I find a constant delight, strange women whom I first took into my house as her handmaids become her rivals, and absorb a portion of my time." Among these "strange women" medicine took a foremost position. Alfadhel placed the name of Maimonides on the list of royal physicians, bestowed an annual salary upon him, and loaded him with distinctions. Maimonides shows less originality than learning in his medical works; he relied on precedent, and was noted for his familiarity with the older authorities. His medical writings, all of which are composed in Arabic, are for the most part summaries or elaborations of Galen, "the Medical Oracle of the Middle Ages." His medical aphorisms, in the judgment of Graetz, "contain nothing further than extracts and classifications of older theories." Yet this does incomplete justice to our hero. Maimonides certainly used experience as well as precedent as his guide; he tested his remedies by actual experiment; he

recognised how deeply physical conditions are
affected by psychic causes, and maintained,
with a strong touch of modernity, that the
aim of the doctor is to prevent illness more
than to cure it. It was in times of health
that the patient might most effectively prepare to meet and conquer the assaults of
disease. Abd-el-Latif, the famous Bagdad
physician, who stayed in Cairo for ten years
(1194–1204), asserted that his visit to Egypt
was in part due to his anxiety to see three men
there, among them Musa ben Maimon. "The
poet and khadi, Alsaid ibn Sina Almulk," adds
Graetz, "sang of Abu-Amram's (Maimonides')
greatness as a doctor in ecstatic verse :—

Galen's art heals only the body,
But Abu-Amram's the body and soul.
He could heal with his wisdom the sickness of
  ignorance.
If the moon would submit to his art,
He would deliver her of her spots at the time of
  full moon,
Complete for her, her periodic defects,
And at the time of her conjunction restore her
  from her waning." [69]

The fall of Jerusalem into Saladin's hands
in 1187 reopened the Holy City to the Jews.[70]
Saladin freely permitted Zion's eldest sons to
settle there, and they blithely availed them-

selves of the opportunity. It was long before
the Jewish population attained large dimen-
sions, but the growth of the new Jerusalem
dates from the resumption of Moslem supremacy. Maimonides had suffered in spirit
when in 1165 he beheld the desolation of
Jerusalem, and it may well be that to his
influence with Saladin were due the privileges
now conferred on his brethren. Saladin,
the nobility of whose character has not been
exaggerated by Lessing or Scott, needed little
persuasion. Just as he welcomed the desire
of Christian priests to hold services in the
Church of the Holy Sepulchre, so he held
out his friendly hand to Jews who longed
to worship at the sites sacred to their past.
During the brief years of Saladin's personal
rule, Jerusalem first justified the claim it
still enjoys—the claim to the fulfilment of the
Hebrew prophet's dream : "My house shall
be called a house of prayer to all peoples."

The Vizir Alfadhel is said at this period
to have saved Maimonides from a serious
danger. Maimonides was now the official
head of the Jewish community, " Nagid "
37.* (Prince) over the whole Egyptian Jewry.
He used his position for public not for
private gain. He accepted no salary for himself, but turned his influence to good account.
Yemen, the much-enduring, felt a lighter

yoke when Maimonides, at the head of Jewish
affairs, had the ear of the Vizir and the Vizir's
master. But the very prominence of Maimonides' position exposed him to risks which
he had little foreseen. That Samuel ben Ali
of Bagdad should become embittered as his
rival progressed is intelligible ; but another
danger now threatened. Among our hero's
friends in Fez had been Abul-Arab ibn Moisha.
When the latter came to Cairo from the
Maghreb, he recognised in the head of the
Jewish community the man whom he had
taken in past years for a Moslem. The
Vizir had no difficulty in acquitting Maimonides of the charge of apostasy now preferred against him. The whole story is too
circumstantial to be lightly rejected as inaccu-
rate.[71] Alfadhel's regard for Maimonides was
quite strong enough to carry our hero through
a fiercer storm. As we shall see, Maimonides
was so trusted and admired at Alfadhel's
court that he had to pay daily visits to it.
Engaged in communal affairs, with a large
practice as a doctor, Maimonides was nevertheless able to occupy himself in his theological studies. During these years, while
the Holy War was raging, Maimonides was
engaged on the third and last of his great
works, the treatise which was to set the
crown on his reputation.

CHAPTER X

"The Guide of the Perplexed"

(1190)

IN all his previous works Maimonides had touched upon philosophical questions. He held that the Scriptures were not only a guide to conduct, but that they contained, enveloped in a more or less allegorical wrapping, the essence of all metaphysical truth. If the ordinary Jew had lost hold of this metaphysic, it was because "barbarians deprived us of our possessions, put an end to our science and literature, killed our wise men, and thus we have become ignorant" (*Guide*, II. c. xi.). Maimonides more than once makes this claim, and Jewish authors have not been the only ones to maintain that Greek Philosophy was a derivative from Hebraic inspiration.[72] Even Aristotle, the legend goes, accompanied his pupil Alexander the Great to Jerusalem, and obtaining possession

of the original works of King Solomon, utilised them in developing his own system.
Though, however, Maimonides contended that
philosophy was the heritage of Israel, he had,
in his treatment of such subjects in his earlier
books, never forgotten that to the generality
even of learned readers the technique of
metaphysics was strange. He now felt that
he also owed a duty to a class of students
other than " unlettered tyros," and in whom
a " previous knowledge of logic and natural
philosophy " might be presupposed (*Introd.*).
" My theory aims at pointing out a straight
way, at casting up a high-road. Ye who have
gone astray in the field of the Holy Law,
come hither and follow the path which I have
prepared. The unclean and the fool shall
not pass over it. It shall be called the Way
of Holiness." [73]

That " Metaphysics cannot be made popular "
is the subject of a whole chapter of the
Guide (I. xxxiv.). Maimonides enumerates
five reasons why it is undesirable " to instruct
the multitude in pure metaphysics." The
subject itself is difficult. " He who can swim
may bring up pearls from the depth of the
sea ; he who cannot swim will be drowned."
Again, though every man possesses perfection
in potentia, it does not follow that every one
can realise this potentiality. Thirdly, the pre-

liminary studies (including geometry, astronomy, physics, and logic) are of long duration, and "man in his natural desire to reach the goal finds them frequently too wearisome. . . . He who approaches metaphysical problems without due preparation is like a mān who starts on a journey and falls into a pit. He had better remain at home." But it is not intellectual preliminaries alone that are required. There are, fourthly, moral qualifications which include a seasoned integrity, moderation, and humility. Such qualities are incompatible with the heat of youth. Hence a certain age is required before the study of metaphysics is advisable. Finally, most men are too occupied with the concerns of the world to acquire philosophical taste and aptitudes. "For these reasons it was proper that the study of metaphysics should have been exclusively cultivated by privileged persons, and not entrusted to the common people. Such studies are not for the beginner, and he should abstain from them, just as the little child must abstain from solid food and from carrying heavy weights." [74]

In Joseph Aknin Maimonides felt that he had a disciple worthy of receiving his fullest confidence. He tells Aknin in his Prefatory Epistle : "Your absence has prompted me to compose this treatise for you and for those

who are like you, however few they may
be." Even so, the author hesitated very
much before writing his *Guide* for "thinkers
whose studies brought them into collision
with religion," yet, he adds, "When I find
the road narrow, and can see no other way
of teaching a well-established truth except by
pleasing one intelligent man and displeasing
ten thousand fools, I prefer to address myself
to the one man, and to take no notice whatever of the condemnation of the multitude."
To Aknin, then, he sent the *Guide*, chapter
by chapter, as he completed each in Arabic.
The book was, as the author himself remarks,
a supplement to his *viva voce* lessons to Aknin
(ii. 24). The perplexities to which Maimonides
directed himself were not those of sceptics, but
of believers ; men firm in their religious faith,
yet bewildered " on account of the ambiguous
and figurative expressions employed in the
Scriptures." In a sense the problem before
Maimonides was the same that faced the
Christian scholastics, that faces all men who
cannot but serve the two masters, Reason
and Faith. But the scholastics of the twelfth
century took two lines equally far from that
taken by Maimonides. Some of them de-
posed Reason from her throne, and made her
the handmaid of Faith. Others simply sub-
stituted Athens for Rome, and set up Aristotle

in place of the Pope. Maimonides trusted
Reason completely, but he rendered no slavish
worship to Aristotle. Spinoza accuses him of
disingenuousness in asserting that he could
always find in Scripture the truths which reason
revealed ; that, when his philosophy contra-
dicted the plain utterance of the Bible, he
would not therefore suspect the former, but
would seek for a new interpretation of the
latter.[75]   No doubt Maimonides does confess
that he was guided by this principle in his
reconciliation of theology with metaphysics.
"I do not reject the Eternity of the Universe," says Maimonides (ii. 25), " *because* certain passages in Scripture confirm the Creation ;
for such passages are not more numerous than
those in which God is represented as a corporeal being ; nor is it impossible or difficult
to find for them a suitable interpretation."
"Those passages in the Bible, which, in their
literal sense, contain statements that can be
refuted by proof, must and can be interpreted
otherwise."   But Maimonides simply perceived that certain passages in Scripture *must*
either be allegorised or pronounced false ; he
preferred the former to the latter alternative.
"Employ your reason," he says (ii. 47), "and
you will be able to discern what is said alle-
gorically, figuratively, and hyperbolically, and
what is meant literally, exactly according to

the original meaning of the words. You
will then understand all prophecies, learn and
retain rational principles of faith, pleasing in
the eyes of God, who is most pleased with
truth, and most displeased with falsehood ;
your mind and heart will not be so perplexed
as to believe or accept as law what is untrue
or improbable, while *the Law is perfectly true
when properly understood.*" (Very much of
Maimonides' allegorising is, let it be noted,
based on perfectly sound exegesis. " Every
prophet has his own peculiar diction" (ii. 29)
is a true generalisation.) But how comes it
that the Scriptures need an esoteric explanation ? Because the Word of God was designed for all men, for simple believers as well
as for men whose faith was reinforced by
philosophy. The Bible has its message for
both. On the one hand, in Rabbinic phrase,
" The Law speaks the language of man," and
its object is to serve for the instruction of
" the young, of women, and of the common
people." But, on the other hand, " Faith
consists in inmost conviction, not in mere
utterances. . . . Faith is apprehension by the
soul " (i. 50). It is possible even for men
" to declare the Unity with their lips, and
assume plurality in their hearts," if their
reason has not come to the aid of their faith
by philosophically analysing the meaning of

Unity. "Show me thy way that I may *know* thee, that I may find grace in thy sight" (Exod. xxxiii. 13), said Moses; and Maimonides comments thus : "We learn from these words that God is known by his attributes, for Moses believed that he knew him, when he was shown the ways of God. The words, 'that I may know thee,' &c., imply that he who knows God will find grace in his eyes. Not only is he acceptable and welcome to God, who fasts and prays, but every one who acquires a knowledge of him" (i. 54). Maimonides believed, but with the mind as well as the heart. "In this manner," he concludes one of his characteristic allegorisations, "will those understand the dark sayings of the prophets who desire to understand them, who awake from the sleep of forgetfulness, deliver themselves from the sea of ignorance, and raise themselves upward nearer to higher things. But those who prefer to swim in the waters of their ignorance, and to go down very low, need not exert the body or heart; they need only cease to move and they will go down by the law of nature" (ii. 10). If this was the scholastic attitude, it was the attitude of Erigena rather than of Abelard. Maimonides was not a reconciler of two distinct bodies of truths—he was a unifier. Reason and Faith taught one

truth. And though we may now differ from
Maimonides in our reading of the message delivered on the one hand by revelation, and
on the other by reason, we have still to thank
him for introducing into Judaism the spirit of
fearless intellectual freedom wedded to severe
moral discipline. It is sometimes amusing
and even painful to observe the desire of
Maimonides to read his own thoughts into
ancient books. " Consider," he remarks in
one place (i. 70), " how these excellent and
true ideas, comprehended only by the
greatest philosophers, are found scattered
in the Midrashim." Yet it was impossible
for a man to go further in defiance of
mere authority than he did, unless he was
prepared like Spinoza to discard authority
altogether.[76]

This favourable view of the attitude of
Maimonides is confirmed by his relations to
Aristotle. Strange as the statement may
appear with reference to a schoolman and
Aristotelian, no man was ever less a slave
to prejudice and preconceptions than he
essentially (though not consistently) was. In
several passages his indignation breaks out
against the men who dare to assert nothing
for which they cannot quote chapter and
verse. Observe, for instance, his relations to
the Arabian Mutakallemim—the Philoso-

phers of the *Kalam* or Word—with whom he
held important points in common. He differed from them in rejecting the atomic
theory, the impossibility of the existence of
substance without accidents, the denial of the
infinite, the untrustworthiness of the senses.
Against all of these doctrines he protested
vigorously and successfully. But when he
agreed with the exponents of the *Kalam* as
he did on the question of Creation (he, with
them, holding the *Creatio ex nihilo* against
Aristotle who maintained the Eternity of the
Universe), such agreement with the Mutakallemim does not moderate his onslaught
against their method, for it is their *method*
rather than their *results* which he is determined to demolish. They made the existence
of God dependent on Creation; and thus
Aristotelians denying Creation would thereby
overthrow the doctrine of the existence of
God. Maimonides accordingly prefers to
adopt for argument's sake the belief in the
eternity of the universe, and to prove on that
basis the existence and unity of God; he
then returns on his premiss, and proves Creation. If the latter is admitted, the existence
of God follows, for a Creation presupposes a
Creator. It may well be that Maimonides
was partly led to follow this course by a
latent sense that his proofs of Creation were

but imperfectly conclusive. But his opposition to the method of the Kalam must be given in his own words, for it will be clearly seen that the utterer of these remarks was no ordinary scholastic. His hostility to the Mutakallemim arose because "first of all they considered what must be the properties of things which should yield proof for or against a certain creed ; and when this was found, they asserted that the thing must be endowed with these properties. . . . They found in ancient books strong proofs for the acceptance or rejection of certain opinions, and thought there was no further need to discuss them " (i. 71). Maimonides did not accept the Ptolemaic astronomy as final or perfect (ii. 24). With regard to Aristotle, the revolt of Maimonides is even more remarkable. He differs from him on the Creation controversy, but more than that. He casts ridicule on those "who blindly follow " the Greek philosopher—who " consider it wrong to differ from Aristotle, or to think that he was ignorant or mistaken in anything" (ii. 15). It would be difficult to match this independence in other schoolmen of his age, and hence it is that despite the obsolete nature of many of the problems to which Maimonides directs himself in the *Guide*, his treatise breathes a modern spirit, or rather a spirit which responds to the intellectual necessities of all ages.

It would be unprofitable to offer a full analysis of the contents of the *Guide*. The spirit of the book is immortal, but much of its actual content is obsolete. Thus one of the main objects of the work is to explain certain terms occurring in the Bible, to bring its anthropomorphic expressions into relation with the true theory of the nature of God. Mohammedan critics had energetically attacked Judaism on this ground, urging that its conception of God was degraded by the application of corporeal attributes to Him.[77] The true reply to this, that the Bible enshrines expressions dating from different strata of religious belief, and that the final message of the Hebrew Scriptures is to be found in its highest and purest ideas, not in its more primitive and popular phraseology, was impossible to Maimonides and his age, though it is remarkable how near Maimonides approached to the modern view in some points. Earlier Jewish philosophers and theologians had explained these corporeal expressions as figurative, but Maimonides is not satisfied with this : he attempts to assign to each of them some definite metaphysical meaning. Thus the narrative of Adam's sin is interpreted as an allegorical exposition of the

relations between Sensation, Intellect, and the Moral Faculty. Adam originally possessed in perfection the intellectual faculty by which he distinguished between the *true* and the *false* qualities inherent in the things themselves. His sin lowered this intellectual faculty, and his passions being no longer under its control, the moral idea of *good* and *evil* replaced the intellectual contrast of *true* and *false* ; for morality restrains the desires and appetites which only come into play when the supremacy of the intellect is weakened or overthrown. Adam, Eve, and the Serpent, represent the intellect, the body, and the imagination. Adam's three sons typify the three elements in man : the vegetable, the animal, and the intellectual. Abel and Cain perish, but Seth (the intellect) survives and forms the basis of the human race (ii. 30, 31).

Maimonides proceeds to show, soundly enough, that ordinary men consider matter or body the only true and full existence ; that which is neither itself a body nor a force resident in a body, is to such men non-existent and inconceivable. Again, life is commonly identified with motion, although motion is not a part of the essence but a mere accident of life. Perception, again, is the most conspicuous means of acquiring knowledge. Especially is this true of sight and hearing, while language is the only mode of communication between one mind and another. Hence, says Maimonides, the God of the Bible who "rides on *araboth*" (*i.e.* presides over the highest sphere of immaterial things), and is identical with the Primal Cause and Ever-active Intellect of the philosophers—this God is described in Scripture as acting, seeing, hearing, and speaking, and even the organs by which those functions are performed in man are ascribed to Him ; for in man those functions are perfections, and they are predicated of God because we wish to assert His perfection. Yet Attributes are, according to Maimonides, utterly inapplicable to God. We cannot even predicate His *essence ;* we can only assert *that* He exists. No definition of God is possible *per genus et differentiam*, since these are the causes of the existence of anything so defined, and God is the final cause. Even Unity is inadmissible as an accident to God ; God is One, but does not possess the attribute of Unity. To say in the usual meaning of the term that God is One, is to imply that His essence is susceptible of quantity ; but, as metaphysics is forced to employ inadequate language, in order to assert that God *does not include a plurality*, we declare that He is One. Hence, since only *negative* attributes

are admissible, and since these are infinite
in number, there is no possibility of obtaining
a knowledge of the true essence of God.
Yet, paradoxically enough, Maimonides holds
that the greater the number of the negative
attributes one can rationally assign, the
nearer one has reached to a knowledge
of God.[78]

This leads us to consider an important
part of Maimonides' philosophy, *viz.*, the
meaning of communication between God and
man. In passing at once to his theory of
prophecy, we are omitting his proofs of the
Existence of God. For the latter purpose,
he enunciates (Part ii.) twenty-six proposi-
tions, which are an admirable summary of the
Aristotelian metaphysics. He holds these pro-
positions inadequate, and proceeds to adduce
his own proofs for the existence of an "infinite, incorporeal, and uncompounded Primal
Cause. The series of causes for every
change is finite, and terminates in the Primal
Cause." This remains the most acceptable
proof of the existence of God. Again, as
regards *Creatio ex nihilo.* The Universe is
a living, organic being, of which the earth
is the centre. There are obvious points of
contact between this view and modern scientific theory, a view which is as far from
materialism on the one hand as from Pan·

theism on the other. Over and over again
Maimonides, amid the most obsolete of medieval metaphysics, strikes an eternally vital
chord. He continues to argue that all life
and change in the Universe depend upon
the revolutions of the Spheres, each of which
has its Soul and Intellect (the Scriptural
Angels are identical with the Intellects of
the Spheres). This well accords with Aristotle, but Maimonides parts company with
his master when the latter holds that these
Spheres and Intellects coexist with the Primal
Cause. Faithful to the Scriptural view,
Maimonides maintains that the Spheres and
their Intellects had a beginning, and were
brought into existence by the will of the
Creator. He derives the doctrine of *Creatio
ex nihilo* from this theory as to the creation
of the spheres. "Admitting that the great
variety of the things in the sublunary world
can be traced to those immutable laws which
regulate the influence of the spheres on the
beings below—the variety in the spheres can
only be explained as the result of God's
free will." [79]

As to the divine communication with man
(ii. 32 *seq.*), Maimonides agrees with the Platonic or general Greek view that *prophecy* or
attainment of direct knowledge of the truth is
a *natural* faculty of men which may be reached

by all who submit to the necessary preparation, and who can raise themselves to the
requisite intellectual and moral perfection.
Maimonides endeavours to show that this is
also the view of the Bible, but he is not
successful in the attempt, and most of his
Jewish successors have severely attacked him
on this point.   He seeks to anticipate obvious
objections by declaring that men duly qualified
may be withheld from prophecy by the will
of God.   But in reply to this one must urge
that according to Scripture the will of God
is the regular and normal condition for acquiring the prophetic spirit.   Prophecy, in the
view of Maimonides, is an emanation through
the Active Intellect to man's rational and
imaginative faculty, *i.e.* the faculty of receiving sense-impressions, and retaining and
combining images of them.   The latter part
of the faculty is most active in dreams, which
differ from prophetic vision in degree and not
in kind.   The imagination (in the psychological meaning of the term) acquires such
an efficiency in its action that it regards the
image as if it came from without, and as
if it were perceived through the bodily senses.
Granted that a man possess a brain and body
in perfect health, that his passions are pure
and well balanced, that his thoughts are
engaged in lofty matters, that his attention

is directed to the knowledge of God—such a man must be a prophet. If he be of the highest order, his imagination will represent things not previously perceived by the senses, which his intellect will have been perfect enough to comprehend. Maimonides' view seems to come to this, that prophecy does not differ essentially from ordinary intellection : perception is *always* the result of a divine influence, and prophecy is that state of intellection in which the preliminary *sense*-perception is more or less dispensed with ; in a word, when the divine influence, by acting immediately on the perfect intellect, is (psychologically speaking) represented by the perfect imagination, without the intermedia-39.* tion of the faulty and defective senses.

By this and other original conceptions, too technical to reproduce here, Maimonides introduced a fresh spirit into Jewish theology. God was realised in thought as in action ; and the Law of God became at once a guide to conduct, and a rational bond between the human and the divine. In the third part of the *Guide* Maimonides insists again and again that the purpose of the Law is man's perfection. "The well-being of the soul is promoted by correct opinions . . . the well-being of the body is established by a proper control of the relations of practical life."

"The Guide of the Perplexed"

The Law aims at producing this "double
perfection" of man. In his investigation of
the origins of certain precepts of the Law,
Maimonides adopts a modern standpoint:
his importance in the scientific study of
religion has not yet been fully realised.
There are few parallels in the twelfth
century to his interest in other forms of
religion, his appreciation of the value of
primitive ideas in explaining the developed
theology of Israel. He is less admirable in
his attempt to derive the food laws of the
Pentateuch from hygienic and medical
principles, for his theory explains only a
part of the facts. Whatever the primitive
origin of the dietary code, it is, in the
Pentateuch, a detail of the great law of
"holiness," which includes within its range
both spirit and body, and makes for that
very "double perfection" of which Maimonides himself speaks in other connections.
No part of the *Guide*, again, led to more
controversy than his theory as to Sacrifices [80]
(III. chs. xxxii. and xlvi.). Here Maimonides
collects many facts as to sacrificial rites
among other peoples, proves the general
prevalence and affection for this method
of worship, and argues that in the Pentateuch
sacrifices were a concession rather than an
ordinance. "It was in accordance with the

wisdom and plan of God, as displayed in
the whole Creation, that He did not command us to discontinue all these manners of
service ; for to obey such a commandment,
would have been contrary to the nature of
man, who generally cleaves to that to which
he is used. It would in those days have
made the same impression as a prophet would
make at present if he called us to the service
of God and told us in His name that we
should not pray to Him, nor fast, nor seek
His help in time of trouble ; that we should
serve Him in thought and not by any action "
(III. xxxii.). This is the theory of Maimonides,
the individual thinker. It is not inconsistency,
still less dishonesty, that made Maimonides, as
a codifier, include in his *Mishneh Torah* the
restoration of the Sacrifices among the tenets
of traditional Judaism.

Apart, then, from any specific contri-
butions to religious thought, the *Guide* is a
permanent influence in Judaism, an influence
entirely for good. True, every age has its
own perplexities and needs its own Guide.
But the spirit of Maimonides may help us
now as it helped sympathetic souls in the
twelfth century. The scholastic theory that
spirit and mind are one, that God reveals
Himself in nature, in man, and in His
Word, that philosophy and faith lead equally

to truth and to the same truth, that religion
to be a force in life must satisfy its intellectual
as well as its moral and emotional necessities,
that he lives unto God who lives unto truth,
—this great and abiding conception finds its
culmination in the *Guide* of Maimonides.
All further development in Judaism starts
with and from the *Guide*. Its logic may no
longer satisfy, its metaphysics no longer suffice,
but its spirit must be with us if we would
serve God as He would be served, if the
knowledge of God is to fill the earth as the
waters cover the seas. "The highest kind
of worship," says Maimonides as he
approaches the end of his treatise, "is only
possible when the knowledge of God has
been acquired. . . . The fear of God is
produced by the *practices* prescribed in the
Law ; the love of God is the result of the
truths taught in the Law. . . . That perfection in which man can truly glory is
attained by him when—as far as this is
possible for man—he has acquired the knowledge of God, of His providence. . . . With
this knowledge to help him he will deter-
minedly seek loving-kindness, judgment, and
righteousness, and thus *imitate the ways of God.*
. . . May He grant us, and all Israel with us to
attain that which He promised us : ' The
eyes of the blind shall be opened, and the

ears of the deaf shall be unstopped'; 'the people that walked in darkness have seen a great light ; they that dwell in the land of the shadow of death, upon them hath the light shined' (Isaiah xxxv. 5 ; ix. 2)." Then, as though to show that this light, far from being the privilege of the philosophical few, may after all enter into the heart of all men, Maimonides closes the *Guide* with these words :—

"God is near to all that call upon Him, if they call upon Him in truth, and turn to Him. He is found by every one who seeks Him, if he, the seeker, goes steadfastly towards Him, nor ever turns astray. AMEN."

CHAPTER XI

Last Years

(1193–1204)

WITH the completion of the *Guide* the life-work of Maimonides was ended. He was then only fifty-five, and had another fourteen years to live, but his health was broken and his strength was absorbed by his professional work as Nagid of the Jewish community and as Physician of the Court. Cairo, moreover, passed through troublous times, and Maimonides must have been affected by the political anxieties of the government.[81] On the death of Saladin in 1193, dissension prevailed among the Sultan's family, despite the prudent counsels of Saladin's brother, el-Adil ("Saphadin"). Saladin's son 'Aziz, who had succeeded to the Egyptian throne, died in 1198 from a fever caught during a hunting expedition in the Fayyum, and el-Adil became master not only of Egypt but of the greater

Maimonides

part of Saladin's empire. In 1201 the Nile
was exceptionally low, and famine and pesti-
lence ravaged Egypt. The account given
of the consequent distress by the Bagdad
physician, 'Abd-el-Latif (who, as has been
mentioned before, was in Cairo from 1194–
1204), is terrible in the extreme. He asserts
that from end to end of Egypt the inhabitants
habitually ate human flesh, and that the
"very graves were ransacked for food."

But 'Abd-el-Latif is given to exaggeration.
"As a whole," says Mr. Lane Poole, "the
period of Ayyubid rule in Egypt, in point
of imperial power, internal prosperity, and
resolute defence against invasion, stands pre-
eminent in the history of the country." [82] El-
Latif passes the bound again when he says
that during this very period Maimonides, "a
man of very high merit," was "governed by
an ambition to take the first place, and to make
himself acceptable to men in power." Maimonides certainly did not lack ambition, and
he does adopt, especially in the *Guide*, a
"superior air" towards all but the philosophical clique. The suspicion of Efodi
that the contrast drawn at the end of *Guide*
between light and darkness refers to the
period after and before the composition of
the *Guide*, seems, however, unfounded.
Maimonides' irritating assumption of con-

140

fidence in his own views, his conviction that
only those could differ from him who failed
to understand him — these were as much
literary fashions as is the conventional
humility of modern writers. Even less just
is el-Latif's charge that Maimonides aimed
at the favour of the great. Admired by the
great, Maimonides was worshipped by the
masses, and he deserved the applause of the
few and of the many. His time was, as we
shall see, at the disposal of the poor as well as
of the rich, and if he became the favourite of
rulers, he was none the less the idol of the
ruled. But he never sought or won popular
affection ; he was too detached from the
emotions of the many for the many to regard
him with emotion. He was out of sympathy
with the "play" side of human nature.
Poetry, though he occasionally lapses into a
flowery style in his own epistles, he held
a childish waste of time,[83] music had no
charms for him ; eating and drinking and
love were to him justifiable only in so
far as necessary for maintaining the life of
the individual or continuing the race. Ibn
Gabriol might sing of the joys of wine,
Abraham Ibn Ezra might versify the praises of
chess, Jehuda Halevi might turn his poetical
genius to the idealisation of human love.
The pleasures of the table were to Maimonides

a degradation ; to sing of love was to use a
divine gift in an act of rebellion against the
giver. Maimonides, both in his *Guide* and
in his medical precepts drawn up for the
Vizir, directed himself against *excess* in all of
these things, but he can have had no fondness
for them even in moderation. Still, his view
of life was not ascetic ; it was purely intellectual. His God was a metaphysical entity
who must be approached with morality and
piety, but also with philosophical understanding. Few were the elect, in this view. But
the virility, the sanity of the view is undeni-
able. Maimonides enthroned God in the
most abiding of thrones, the human Reason.
If God is firmly seated there, the heart is also
moved towards and by the divine spirit ; but
a religion which *originates* in the emotions
ends in sensuousness or mysticism. Religion
is, after all, an emotion, but in a pure,
spiritual monotheism such as Maimonides
expounded, the fount of this emotion is in
the reason, not in the senses.

At the moment when his *Guide* was
finished, the opposition of the Gaon in Bagdad reached its severest phase.[84] It was thus
that he found himself compelled to explain
in a separate Epistle (*Techiyath Hamethim*,
"The Resurrection of the Dead ") his views
on Resurrection. His pupil, Aknin, asked

him to write on the subject.[85] He expressed
his displeasure at being forced to repeat what
he had previously written, and emphatically
asserted that his spiritual view of immortality
did not imply a denial of the return of the
soul to the body. On the other hand, the
opposition of Bagdad was more than balanced
by the appreciation of southern France.
"Nowhere did Maimuni's ideas find a more
fruitful ground," writes Graetz, "and nowhere were they adopted with more readiness
than in the Jewish congregations of South
France, where prosperity, the free form of
government, and the agitation of the Albi-
genses against austere clericalism, had
awakened a taste for scientific investigation,
and where Ibn Ezra, the Tibbon and the
Kimchi families, had scattered seeds of Jewish
culture. . . . Not only laymen, but even
profound Talmudists, like Jonathan Cohen
of Lunel, idolised him, eagerly watched for
every word of his, and paid him homage.
'Since the death of the last authority of the
Talmud, there has never been such a man in
Israel.'"   The last years of Maimonides
were sweetened by the correspondence which
ensued between himself and the Provençal
Jews. These regarded him as more than
human, as the instrument divinely appointed
for the revival and purification of Judaism.

They consulted him in their doubts, and
drew from him some very notable letters. In
1194 he detailed, in reply to questions from
Marseilles, his views on astrology. His letter
is remarkable for its era, and takes its place
worthily by the side of Ibn Ezra's protest
against a belief in demons. "Know, my
masters," writes Maimonides, "that no man
should *believe* anything which is not attested
by one of these three sanctions : Rational
proof, as in mathematical sciences ; the perception of the senses ; or tradition from the
prophets and the righteous." Works on
astrology were the product of fools, who
mistook vanity for wisdom. Men were
inclined to believe whatever was written in a
book, especially if the book were ancient ; and
in olden times disaster befell Israel because
men devoted themselves to such idolatry
instead of practising the arts of martial
defence and government. He had himself
studied every extant astrological treatise, and
had convinced himself that they did not
deserve to be called scientific. Maimonides
then proceeds to distinguish between astrology
and astronomy, in the latter of which lies
true and necessary wisdom. He ridicules
the supposition that the fate of man could be
dependent on the constellations, and urges
that such a theory robs life of purpose, and

makes man a slave of destiny. "It is true," he concludes, "that you may find stray utterances in the Rabbinical literature which imply a belief in the potency of the stars at a man's nativity, but no one is justified in surrendering his own rational opinions because this or that sage erred, or because an allegorical remark is expressed literally. A man must never cast his own judgment behind him ; the eyes are set in the front, not in the back."   43.*

Jonathan of Lunel has already been named among the ardent admirers of Maimonides. He now sent to Cairo a series of twenty-four questions on points arising out of the *Mishneh Torah*. Some time elapsed before Maimonides could find leisure to reply, and he did so in a letter pathetic with its picture of weariness and weakness. The same note is struck in the letter which he sent to Samuel Ibn Tibbon, who was engaged in a Hebrew translation of the *Guide*. From Lunel had come the request that Maimonides would himself undertake the translation. He, however, was well satisfied as to Ibn Tibbon's qualifications, and referred them to the latter. In this epistle he exhorts the Provençal Jews to remain steadfast in their devotion at once to the Talmud and to its scientific study. The despondency of the writer is not more marked than is his

confidence in the saving power of the few.
" You, members of the congregation of Lunel,
and of the neighbouring towns, stand alone in
raising aloft the banner of Moses. You
apply yourselves to the study of the Talmud,
and also cherish wisdom. But in the East
the Jews are dead to spiritual aims. In the
whole of Syria none but a few in Aleppo
occupy themselves with the *Torah* according
to the truth, but even they have it not much
at heart. In Irak there are only two or three
grapes (men of insight); in Yemen and the
rest of Arabia they know little of the Talmud,
and are merely acquainted with Agadic exposition. Only lately have they purchased
copies of my Code, and distributed them
among a few circles. The Jews of Judea
know little of the *Torah*, much less of the
Talmud. Those who live among the Turks
and Tartars have the Bible only, and live
according to it alone. In the Maghreb you
know what is the position of the Jews. Thus
it remains to you alone to be a strong support
to our religion. Therefore be firm and of
good courage, and be united in it." The
letter to Samuel Ibn Tibbon, written in September 1199, opens with a eulogy of Samuel's
father, Judah.[86] " I did not know that he
had left a son. . . . Blessed be He who has
granted a recompense to your learned father,

and granted him such a son ; and indeed not
to him alone, but to all wise men. For in
truth unto us all a child has been born, unto
us all a son has been given. 'This offspring
of the righteous is a tree of life,' a delight of
our eyes, and pleasant to look upon. I have
already tasted of his fruit, and lo, it was sweet
in my mouth even as honey." Maimonides
proceeds to praise Ibn Tibbon's Hebrew
style and his knowledge of Arabic, surprising
as displayed by one born among the " stam-
merers." The Provençal Jews seem to have
spoken and written Arabic faultily. Maimonides' praise of Ibn Tibbon's style is not
generally shared by readers of his translations.
But whether Ibn Tibbon fulfilled Maimonides' ideal or not, the Cairo sage formulates
an excellent canon for his correspondent's
guidance. " Let me premise one canon.
Whoever wishes to translate, and purposes to
render each word literally, and at the same
time to adhere slavishly to the order of the
words and sentences in the original, will
meet with much difficulty. This is not the
right method. The translator should first
try to grasp the sense of the subject
thoroughly, and then state the theme with
perfect clearness in the other language. This,
however, cannot be done without changing
the order of words, putting many words for

one word, or *vice versa*, so that the subject be
perfectly intelligible in the language into
which he translates." Maimonides then
enters *seriatim* into Ibn Tibbon's difficulties,
and advises him as to his course of philosophical
reading. But the most interesting passage is
the one in which Maimonides describes his
own manner of life :—

Now God knows that in order to write this to
you, I have escaped to a secluded spot, where
people would not think to find me, sometimes
leaning for support against the wall, sometimes
lying down on account of my excessive weakness,
for I have grown old and feeble.

But with respect to your wish to come here to
me, I cannot but say how greatly your visit would
delight me, for I truly long to commune with you,
and would anticipate our meeting with even greater
joy than you. Yet I must advise you not to
expose yourself to the perils of the voyage, for
beyond seeing me, and my doing all I could to
honour you, you would not derive any advantage
from your visit. Do not expect to be able to
confer with me on any scientific subject for even
one hour either by day or by night, for the following is my daily occupation :—

I dwell at Misr (Fostat) and the Sultan re-
sides at Kahira (Cairo); these two places are two
Sabbath days' journey (about one mile and a half)
distant from each other. My duties to the Sultan
are very heavy. I am obliged to visit him every

day, early in the morning ; and when he or any of
his children, or any of the inmates of his harem,
are indisposed, I dare not quit Kahira, but must
stay during the greater part of the day in the
palace. It also frequently happens that one or two
of the royal officers fall sick, and I must attend to
their healing. Hence, as a rule, I repair to Kahira
very early in the day, and even if nothing unusual
happens, I do not return to Misr until the afternoon. Then I am almost dying with hunger. I
find the ante-chambers filled with people, both
Jews and Gentiles, nobles and common people,
judges and bailiffs, friends and foes—a mixed
multitude, who await the time of my return.

I dismount from my animal, wash my hands, go
forth to my patients, and entreat them to bear with
me while I partake of some slight refreshment,
the only meal I take in the twenty-four hours.
Then I attend to my patients, write prescriptions
and directions for their various ailments. Patients
go in and out until nightfall, and sometimes even, I
solemnly assure you, until two hours and more in
the night. I converse with and prescribe for them
while lying down from sheer fatigue, and when
night falls I am so exhausted that I can scarcely
speak.

In consequence of this, no Israelite can have any
private interview with me except on the Sabbath.
On that day the whole congregation, or at least the
majority of the members, come to me after the
morning service, when I instruct them as to their
proceedings during the whole week ; we study

together a little until noon, when they depart. Some of them return, and read with me after the afternoon service until evening prayers. In this manner I spend that day. I have here related to you only a part of what you would see if you were to visit me.

Now, when you have completed for our brethren the translation you have commenced, I beg that you will come to me, but not with the hope of deriving any advantage from your visit as regards your studies ; for my time is, as I have shown you, excessively occupied.

The end came on December 13, 1204, when Maimonides died in his seventieth year.[87] A general outburst of grief ensued. Public mourning was ordained in many congregations in all parts of the world. For three days Jews and Moslems held lament in Fostat. Maimonides was buried in Palestine, at Tiberias. In Jerusalem a general fast was proclaimed. From the Scroll of the Law was read the passage (Leviticus xxvi.) in which are unfolded the penalties resulting from disobedience to the divine precepts, and from the first Book of Samuel, the narrative of the capture of the Ark of the Covenant by the Philistines, concluding with the words (1 Samuel iv. 22) : " The glory is departed from Israel, for the Ark of God is taken."

CHAPTER XII

The Influence of Maimonides

THE first effect of the life-work of Maimonides was a cleavage in Jewish opinion. But this cleavage was in no sense a disintegration. In the end, both his *Code* and his *Guide* were adopted as text-books by conservatives and liberals alike. Were it not that the cleft between men of simple faith and men given to philosophical apprehension of religion is perennially recurrent, the struggle between Maimonists and anti-Maimonists would strike the modern reader as trivial and obsolete. Though, however, such conflicts are chronic in human life, every age agrees in calm compromise on the doubts that assailed its predecessor, reserving its own excitement for its more immediate problems. Both Maimonists and anti-Maimonists exaggerated their differences. On the one hand were the enthusiastic worshippers of the master who could see truth in him alone ; on the other side stood an equally convinced party of opponents who denounced the teachings of Maimonides as heretical. There were unpleasant features in the struggle, but these and not the good results were ephemeral. The medieval weapon of excommunication was freely used, and the incriminated books were committed to the pyre in an unavailing attempt " to quench the flame of truth with fire." An appeal was made to the secular arm, and Dominicans were invited to decide questions affecting the most intimate concerns of Judaism.

This is ancient history, in the sense that it has left no disfiguring mark. The good that these men did lived after them, the evil was buried with their bones. The triumph of Maimonides was complete all along the line. But the opposite party gained something for which it contended. The philosophical conception of Judaism was allowed a high place in the schools, but Judaism was not merged into Rationalism. This was due to the anti-Maimonists, while the medieval Kabbala (or mysticism) applied to the Jewish religion that touch of emotion which Maimonides so conspicuously lacked. Again, the aim of Maimonides to provide a Code which should form a final court of appeal in Jewish life was unsuccessful. Into Spain itself, the

The Influence of Maimonides

French methods of studying the Talmud were introduced in the century following the death of Maimonides. So far from destroying *pilpul* — casuistical discussion — the *Code* or *Mishneh-Torah* itself became the object of pilpulistic comment. This was to the advantage of Judaism. Pilpul is to law as laboratory work to science.

Despite these facts, it is nevertheless accurate to assert that Maimonides won all along the line. Whereas before his day the philosophical study of Judaism had numbered but a handful of adherents, the band of such students has always been large and powerful since the completion of the *Guide*. If, again, the Kabbala did good, it was because the sane influence of Maimonides prevented the harm which, but for him, might have ensued. For Maimonides not only introduced an intellectual principle. He also applied a spiritualising principle. The grossness, the materialism of medieval religion could not survive the idealism of the *Guide*. Especially in the face of the Kabbala, the antagonism of Maimonides to an anthropomorphic conception of God saved Judaism from succumbing to the alluring, sensuous charms inseparable from mysticism. So, too, the *Code* had a permanent value. Not only has it been the means by which Judaism has become known to Europe, but it supplied to those within the pale a rallying point amid the troubles that were soon to befall the Jewish people. If the *Torah* remained a badge of honour which prevailed over the badge of shame imposed by Innocent III.; if the physical walls of the coming ghetto made no prison for the Jewish spirit; if the varying degrees of persecution applied by local governments failed to produce a permanent disintegration of Judaism into a number of local cults; then to Maimonides and his *Code* belongs a large share of the merit. From the *Mishneh-Torah* to the *Shulchan Aruch*—the Code which now regulates the life of the majority of Jews— the direct genealogical line is unbroken, and though the parent is in many ways superior to the descendant, still the value of the latter as a norm for Jewish life must not be depreciated because its effects have not been all good.

The influence of Maimonides on European thought in general is greater than is usually allowed. It is becoming clearer that the *Guide* was very early known through translations. Apart from this, there is nothing more characteristic of the middle ages than the easy flow of influence between the representatives of various schools and creeds. In the sphere of philosophy, for instance, no distinction can be drawn between Christians, Moslems, and Jews as such. The spirit of Greece enjoyed a threefold revival, leading a new life in Arabic, Latin, and Hebrew.[88] What is more, the three channels often ran together and intermingled, they did not merely start from the same fount. The scholars of the mosque, church, and synagogue worked in the same studies, and some remarkable cases of collaboration might be cited. The books of Jewish writers, known under Latinised names, were often used by Christian students. But we are now dealing only with Maimonides. His biblical exegesis, as expounded in the opening chapters of the *Guide*, was epoch-making, as Professor Bacher has shown.[89] His *Commentary on the Mishnah* gains yearly in repute, and one of the most interesting phenomena of the last quarter of the nineteenth century has been the activity displayed by Jewish scholars in editing the *Siraj*. To return to the *Guide*, Maimonides' doctrine that God cannot be defined attributively, but only negatively, has been of permanent moment in the philosophy of monotheism. His account of the Mohammedan Kalam, with which the first part closes, has been found by scientific historians one of the most useful and keen ex-

aminations of the Islamic after-glow of the
ancient Atomic theories. His rejection of
the Aristotelian doctrine of the eternity of
the world helped Christians to use Aristotle
in their theology.[90] His psychological analysis
of prophecy has worth even for present-day
inquirers.

The *Guide* was written in Arabic, but
in Hebrew characters, and it is said that
the author objected to its transcription into
Arabic script.[91] But we know that such
transcriptions were soon made. 'Abd-el-Latif
read it ; and citations of it are found in the
works of Moslem philosophers. Moslem
commentaries were written on parts of the
Guide ; Moslem teachers lectured on the work
to their students ; and to a Moslem historian
of medicine, Alkifti, the *Guide* represented
the highest product of his age. Of the
translations of the *Guide,* Samuel Ibn Tibbon's is the more noted. It was completed
in Arles in 1204, a fortnight before Maimonides died. Of the influence of this
translation on Jewish thought and on the
language in which that thought expressed
itself, it is impossible to speak with exaggeration. But another translation, that made a
little later by Judah al-Charizi, though in-
ferior in excellence (except in so far as style
is concerned) to Ibn Tibbon's was more im-

The Influence of Maimonides

portant from our present point of view. For
it was from Charizi's Hebrew that the first
Latin translation was made during the first
half of the thirteenth century.[92] Alexander of
Hales, the great Franciscan, who died in   48.*
1245, shows traces of acquaintance with the
Guide, while his contemporary, William of
Auvergne, was even more deeply influenced
by it. From Maimonides, William derived   49.*
his whole knowledge of Judaism. But the
real influence of the *Guide* on Christian
thought begins with the Dominican Albertus
Magnus (died 1280).[93] Albertus Magnus
cited "Moyses Aegyptius," but Maimonides
was more to the Dominican than would
appear from these citations taken alone. As
regards Thomas Aquinas, "his dependence
on Maimonides," says Guttmann,[94] "is not
confined to philosophical details, but in a
certain sense may be detected in the whole
of his theological system." As Emile Saisset
puts it : "Maimonides est le précurseur de
Saint Thomas d'Aquin, et le Moré Nebouk-
him annonce et prépare la summa theologiæ."[95]
If the *Guide* of the Jew and the *Summa* of
the Christian bear this relation, then Maimonides deserves a place among the fathers
of the Church. The Encyclopedist of the
middle ages, Vincent of Beauvais, makes
use of the *Guide* in his *Speculum Majus*.[96]

Duns Scotus, too, knew the *Guide* and held its teachings in esteem.[97] Of the later Latin translations, of the renderings into Castilian, Italian, and other languages of Europe, it is unnecessary to speak. Suffice it to say, in general, that the *Guide*, while it ceased directly to affect European 55.* thought after the age of Descartes, was a potent force in Judaism at various epochs. Elias del Medigo, the first great product of the Italian and Judaic spirit, the teacher of Pico di Mirandola, was inspired by Maimonides ; in Poland, in the sixteenth century, the Jewish revival owed much to the same influence ; in Moses Mendelssohn Maimonides produced an intellectual awakening ; while Isaac Erter, one of the prime movers in the Hebrew renaissance of the nineteenth century, was much affected by the *Guide*.[98] Solomon Maimon, the brilliant, the wayward admirer and critic of the *Guide*, recognised in the man, whose name he adopted, the most powerful influence on his mental development. "My reverence for this great teacher," he writes, "went so far that I regarded him as my ideal of a perfect man. I looked upon his teachings as if they had been inspired with Divine wisdom itself. This went so far that when my passions began to grow, and I had sometimes to fear

158

lest they might seduce me to some action inconsistent with these teachings, I used to employ as a proved antidote the abjuration : ' I swear by the reverence which I owe my great teacher, Rabbi Moses ben Maimon, not to do this act.' And this vow, so far as I can remember, was always sufficient to restrain me." [99]

Spinoza, of whose intellectual relation to Maimonides very opposite views are maintained, paid to the Cairo Rabbi the homage of practical imitation. As Professor Pearson well says : " Maimonides' theory of how a wise man should earn his livelihood seems to me the keynote of Spinoza's life by the optical bench—his refusal of a professorial chair. ' Let,' writes Maimonides, ' thy fixed occupation be the study of the Law, and thy worldly pursuits be of secondary consideration ! ' After stating that all business is only a means to study, in that it provides the necessities of life, he continues : ' He who resolves upon occupying himself solely with the study of the Law, not attending to any work or trade but living on charity, defiles the sacred name and heaps up contumely upon the Law. Study must have active labour joined with it, or it is worthless, produces sin, and leads the man to injure his neighbour. . . . It is a cardinal virtue to live by the work of one's hands, and it is one of the great characteristics of the pious of yore, even that whereby one attains to all respect and felicity of this and the future world.' Why," asks Professor Pearson, "does Spinoza's life stand in such contrast to that of all other modern philosophers? Because his life at least, if not his philosophy, was Hebrew!"[100]

A valuable testimony this to any teacher's influence. Both Solomon Maimon and Spinoza were affected in their lives as well as in their mind by Maimonides, and the same may be said of the Jewish people as a whole. Maimonides taught his brethren how to think; he showed them how to live. Few men have been so little spoiled by success, so little embittered by opposition. Amid praise and blame he stood calm, unflinching. His life was actuated by a consistent purpose. He sowed the ideal, and he won the most priceless of rewards when he in turn became the ideal of many, leading them ever onwards to a higher conception of God and of man's place in the divine universe.

NOTES

1. The account of Cordova, and the history of Andalusia from the reign of Abd-er-Rahman III. (912–961) till 1148 is mainly derived (and in part quoted) from Stanley Lane-Poole's *The Moors in Spain*, London, 1887. See particularly pp. 131, 139, 152, 169, 181, 184.

2. Maimonides gives this pedigree at the end of his *Commentary on the Mishnah*. In Arabic he was called "Abu imran (Amram) Musa ben Maimun abd (Obeid) allah" the Cordovese. Christians cite him as Moses the Egyptian from his subsequent residence in Cairo. His usual Hebrew title is either Maimuni or Rambam, the latter being formed from the initials of *R*abbi *M*oses *b*en *M*aimon (Rabbi Moses the son of Maimon). On his father, Maimon ben Joseph, see, in addition to the usual authorities for the period, L. M. Simmons's Introduction to *The Letter of Consolation of Maimun ben Joseph, edited from the unique Bodleian MS., and translated into English.* (*Jewish Quarterly Review,* 1890, vol. ii. pp. 62 *seq.*) 1.*

3. The "Confession of Faith" of the Almohades, and some of the comments on it, are taken from the English translation contributed by L. M. Simmons to the *Jewish Quarterly Review*, vol. iii. p. 360. The Arabic text was published by I. Goldziher in *ZDMG*, vol. xliv. p. 168.

4. The *best names* "are the ninety-nine attributes of God which Moslems are in the habit of reciting. They are given and translated into English in Palmer's *Qur'an*, vol. i. Introduction lxvii" (*J. Q. R.* iii. 362).

5. Geiger in his *Moses ben Maimon* (*Nachgelassene Schriften*, iii. p. 42) holds that the family of Maimon

161 L

Maimonides

assumed the outward garb of Islam in Spain. The assumption is unfounded. Graetz, who too readily assumes that this occurred later on in Fez, fully acquits Maimon of yielding in Spain. See on this whole question notes 9 and 14 below.

6. On this astronomical work see Steinschneider,
5.* *Hebräische Uebersetzungen*, § 377.

7. Harkavy thinks that it cannot be maintained that Maimonides had no predecessors in commenting on the Mishnah, but as to the originality of Maimonides' method there can be no question (Hebrew ed. of Graetz, iv. Appendix, p. 52).

8. The motive suggested by Sambary (Neubauer, *Medieval Jewish Chronicles*, i. p. 117) is incredible. He states that Maimonides was forced to leave Cordova because of some offensive remarks made by him to the Khalif regarding Moslem rites. Maimonides was too
8.* tolerant to Islam for this story to be admissible.

9. The view expressed in the text seems best to fit the evidence. Geiger, Munk (*Notice sur Joseph ben Jehouda*, 1842, and *Archives Israélites*, 1851, p. 319), and Graetz emphatically maintain that Maimonides actually became a pseudo-Moslem, basing the opinion partly on general considerations, partly on the statements of Arabic authors. The question is fully examined, as to the first class of arguments, by Dr. M. Friedländer (Preface to *Guide of the Perplexed*, vol. i. p. xxxiii), and as to the latter class by Prof. Margoliouth (*Jewish Quarterly Review*, vol. xiii. p. 539). Both vindicate Maimonides against the suspicion that he ever assumed the garb of Islam. See also Lebrecht, *Magazin für die Lit. des Auslandes* (1844, n. 62); H. Kahan's *Hat Moses Maimonides dem Krypto-Mohammedanismus gehuldigt ?* (1899); and Rabbinowitz in the Hebrew ed. of Graetz, vol. iv. pp. 332, 462, and
9.* the references there given.

10. Simmons, *Maimonides and Islam (Jewish Chronicle* Office, 1888), p. 4.

11. On the Arabic text of Maimon's *Letter of Consolation* see note 2 above. A Hebrew translation was published by Goldberg in the *Lebanon*, 1872. The

Notes

citations and some of the comments are taken from Mr. Simmons's English edition. As to the Arabic style of Maimonides in general, and its relation to Moslem Arabic dialects, see I. Friedländer, *Der Sprachgebrauch des Maimonides* (Frankfort, 1902).   10.*

12. Introduction to the *Siraj ; cf.* p. 75.

13. The *Letter concerning Apostasy* was edited by Geiger (Breslau, 1850) and Edelmann (*Chemdah Genuza*, p. 6) ; also in the *Letters* of Maimonides (Leipzig, 1867). *Cf.* Hebrew Graetz, iv. p. 337, n. 1. The authenticity of the Letter has been disputed (see in particular Friedländer, *loc. cit.*), but on the other side, besides Graetz and Geiger, see Simmons's *Maimonides and Islam*, p. 5, and Margoliouth, *loc. cit.* The author must have been a person of consequence, and no one but Maimonides has ever been suggested. The Letter is cited as Maimonides' by Saadiah ibn Danon, Isaac ben Sheshet (*Responsa*, § 11), and Simon ben Zemach Duran (*Responsa*, § 63). The views expressed in the Letter bear a general resemblance to the known views of Maimonides, and there is some striking similarity between the phraseology of this Letter and the incontestably genuine *Iggereth Teman* (see note 36 below). The *Letter concerning Apostasy* by no means implies that Maimonides was himself a pseudo-convert as Munk, Carmoly, and Graetz aver. Prof. Margoliouth rightly says : " The fact of the writer's taking a lenient view of the act of pronouncing the Mohammedan profession of faith, and thinking the matter not one worth dying for, surely need not prove that he had himself followed that course."

14. This is an inference from the course of events ; 11.* without this supposition it is difficult to understand what occurred.

15. See the *Sefer Charedim* of Eleazar Askari of Safed (written in 1588).

16. For the career of Saladin and the history of Egypt in the latter half of the 12th century, two brilliant books by Prof. Stanley Lane-Poole are particularly valuable : (*a*) *Saladin and the Fall of the Kingdom of Jerusalem*, 1898, and (*b*) *A History of Egypt, the Middle Ages*, 1901

Maimonides

(vol. vi. of the *History of Egypt*, edited by Prof. W. M. Flinders Petrie).

17. Maimonides' views on the treatment of the Karaites are derived from his *Responsa*, 71, and *Letters*, 48*b* (ed. Leipzig, §§ 163 and 58).

12.* 18. *Responsa*, § 149.

19. Maimonides' *Letter* to Japhet (note 21 below) ; *cf.* Casici, *Bibliotheca Arabicohispana*, i. 293*a*.

20. See for instance Commentary on *Mishnah Aboth*, iv. 5, on the maxim : " Make not of the Torah a crown wherewith to aggrandise thyself, nor a spade wherewith to dig."

21. This Letter to Japhet, written eight years after the death of his brother David, is published in the Hebrew
13.* Graetz, iv. p. 338, n. 4. In this letter he refers, among other matters, to the dangers he incurred through informers.

22. Lane-Poole, *History of Egypt*, p. 184.

23. A Hebrew version of the general introduction and the first five tractates was made by Charizi, and of the " Eight Chapters " by Samuel ibn Tibbon, but the translation of the whole Commentary was not complete till a century had elapsed (Steinschneider, *Hebräische Uebersetzungen*, p. 923). Since 1523 the Commentary has been printed in numerous editions of the Talmud. Surenhusius translated the Commentary into Latin (1698–1703). Of the original Arabic many parts have now been edited. See Pococke, *Porta Mosis* (1655), Barth (*Makkoth*, 1879–80), Dérenbourg (*Tohoroth*, 1886–92), Baneth (*Aboth*, 1890), Friedländer (*Rosh Hashanah*, 1890), Weil (*Berachoth*, 1891), Bamberger (*Kilajim*, 1891), Zivi (*Demai*, 1891), Weiss (*Sanhedrin*, 1893), Herzog (*Peah*, 1894), Wohl (*Chullin*, iii.–v., 1894), Wiener (*Abodah Zarah*, 1895), Bamberger (*Challah*, 1895), Beermann (*Eduyoth*, i. 1–12, 1897), Löwenstein (*Bechoroth*, 1897), Fromer (*Middoth*, 1898), Holzer (Introduction to *Chelek*, 1901), Behrens (*Megillah*, 1901), Kroner (*Bezah*, 1901), Kroner (*Pesachim*, 1901), Hirschfeld (*Joma*, 1902), Sik (*Taanith*, 1902), Kallner (*Taanith*, i.–ii., 1902), Nurock (*Kiddushin*, 1902), Hamburger (*Introduction*, 1902), J. Simon (*Moed*
15.* *Katan* and *Sabbath*, v.–vii., 1902), M. Fried (*Tamid*, 1903).

Notes

24. In his Introduction to his *Magen Aboth*, a commentary on *Mishnah Aboth*.

25. Weiss, *Dor Dor Vedoreshaw*, iv. 293 ; but contrast the remarks of Rabbinowitz, Hebrew Graetz, iv. p. 341. Frankel's appreciation of Maimonides' Commentary may be found in *Darche Hamishnah*, p. 320. Frankel holds that Maimonides only dissents from the Talmud where the practical law is not affected.

26. Introduction to *Chelek*.

27. Preface to *Guide of the Perplexed*, p. xx.

28. On the *Shemoneh Perakim* ("Eight Chapters"), see Steinschneider, *Hebr. Uebersetz.*, § 254. A Hebrew translation was made by Samuel ibn Tibbon ; the original was edited with a German translation by Wolf (1863). The Hebrew has been often edited. An English translation appeared in the *Hebrew Review* (1835). 16.*

29. Grant, *Ethics of Aristotle*, vol. i. p. 261.

30. Just as Maimonides sought to give an Aristotelian form to Jewish ethics, so Prof. M. Lazarus, in his " Ethics of Judaism," has endeavoured to read into the same ethics the principles of Kant. 17.*

31. The latest edition is J. Holzer's *Mose Maimuni's Einleitung zu Chelek*, 1901. 18.*

32. *Studies in Judaism*, 1896, chapter on " The Dogmas of Judaism."

33. In the prose summary and in the hymn *Yigdal*. See Singer, *Authorised Daily Prayer-Book*, pages 2 and 89. 19.*

34. Lane-Poole, *Saladin*, p. 106.

35. The *Iggereth Teman* was translated into Hebrew thrice : by Samuel ibn Tibbon, Abraham ben Chasdai of Barcelona, and Nahum of the Maghreb. The rendering of the last named is the one mostly printed. Ibn Tibbon's translation appeared in Vienna in 1874. The Letter was written in 1172. 21.*

36. With curious inconsistency the Letter contains a calculation of the same kind that Maimonides condemns. This passage fixes 1216 as the date of the Messianic era ; but this part of the *Letter* is probably spurious (see Friedländer, p. xxiii., *cf.* Hebrew Graetz, p. 348, n. 2). 22.*

Maimonides

23.*   37. Nachmanides in his Letter to the French Rabbis (Frankel's *Monatsschrift*, 1860, 184).

38. *Responsa*, 140, 146.

39. Of the *Responsa* of Maimonides several collections have been published, the edition mostly cited being that issued in Leipzig, 1859. Some facsimiles of the Arabic *Responsa* (with the autograph of Maimonides) were published by G. Margoliouth in the *Jewish Quarterly Review*, vol. xi. p. 533. Geiger published five in the original Arabic (*Melo Chafnaim*, pp. 54–80). On these Arabic *Responsa* compare Simonsen, *Jewish Quarterly Review*, xii. 134. The Hebrew translation is due to Mordecai Tama. One hundred and fifty-five *Responsa* were published in Amsterdam in 1765. The Leipzig edition con-
24.*   tains a larger number, some of doubtful authenticity.

40. *Jewish Quarterly Review*, xi. 536.

25.*   41. *Responsa* (Leipzig), ii. 15.

42. Further extracts from the *Responsa* are given in the Hebrew Graetz, iv. pp. 349 *seq.*

43. *Eben Sappir*, i. 19.

44. *Responsa*, Leipzig, i. 116. For fuller references see Hebrew Graetz, iv. p. 352, n. 1, and Appendix, pp. 51, 54, 55. In marriage contracts the condition as to obedience to the Rabbanite laws of *tebilah* (bathing) was specially added in Egypt. See also *Jewish Quarterly Review* (vol. xiii. 218) for a pre-Maimonist Egyptian marriage settlement. The mutual concessions include that the Rabbanite husband is not to compel his bride to make use of a light on Friday eve, or to profane the festivals according to the Karaite calculation, while the Karaite lady promises on her side to observe also the festivals as fixed by the Rabbanite calendar.

45. Lane-Poole, *History of Egypt*, p. 190.

46. *Ibid.* p. 204. The whole of chapter vii. in Prof. Lane-Poole's *History* has been much utilised.

47. Maimonides himself states (in his Letter to Jonathan of Lunel) that he was occupied for ten years over the *Code*. See Hebrew Graetz, iv. 353, notes 1 and 2, and pp. 462, 466. One of the grounds for selecting the title *Yad Hachazaka* for the *Code*, was the numerical

Notes

coincidence of the Hebrew letters of the word *Yad*
(10 + 4) with the number of the books (14) into which 27.*
the *Code* is divided.

48. The translators of the *Sefer Hamitzvoth* were
Abraham ibn Chasdai, Moses ibn Tibbon, Solomon ibn
Ayyub. See Steinschneider, *Hebr. Uebersetz.*, p. 927.
The Arabic text was published by Bloch, and much help
has been derived from his introduction. His edition
bears the title : *Le Livre des Préceptes par Moïse ben
Maimoun dit Maimonide publié pour la première fois
dans l'original arabe et accompagné d'une introduction et
de notes* (Paris, 1888). Peritz had previously published a
portion of the Arabic in 1882. The Hebrew translation
of Ibn Tibbon is the most often printed.   28.*

49. Maimonides' Letters to Aknin and to Jonathan of
Lunel ; also the introduction to the *Code*. In his Letter
to Phineas ben Meshullam of Alexandria (*Resp.*, 148)
Maimonides disclaims any desire to suppress the study
of the Talmud in the original.

50. On the *Rabad* see Weiss, *op. cit.* iv. p. 300, and
Hebrew Graetz, iv. p. 415.   29.*

51. But an Arabic commentary was written on it. See
*A Muhammadan Commentary on Maimonides' "Mishneh
Torah"* by G. Margoliouth (*Jewish Quarterly Review*, xiii.
488, *cf.* Steinschneider, *ibid.* xii. p. 500). The Mohammedan origin of this Commentary is open to question.

52. This characterisation, together with a good deal
more in the course of the present book, is taken bodily
from Graetz.

53. Letter to Aaron of Lunel ; *cf.* Harkavy in Hebrew
Graetz, iv. p. 55 (n. to p. 368).

54. Letter to Jonathan of Lunel ; Hebrew Graetz, iv.
p. 353, n. 2.

55. *Responsa*, 140.

56. See note 50 above.

57. This view of the conduct of Samuel ben Ali is not
universally accepted. See, on the other side, Harkavy
in Hebrew Graetz. iv , Appendix, pp. 46 and 56. Samuel
according to Harkavy displays much acumen and learning in some of his Responsa, but Maimonides certainly

Maimonides

33.* formed a low estimate of the Exilarch's philosophical attainments, and the view taken by Graetz of the motives of Samuel's opposition to Maimonides seems the true one.

58. Letter to Aknin.

59. The following note is extracted from Dr. Friedländer's edition of the *Guide of the Perplexed*, i. 1 (*cf.* also Hebrew Graetz, iv. 373, n. 1).

Munk in his *Notice sur Joseph Ben-Jehoudah ou Aboul Hadjadj Yousouf Ben-Yahja al Sabti al Maghrebi* (Paris, 1842), described the life of this pupil of Maimonides. The following are the principal facts: Joseph ben Jehudah was born in the Maghreb about the middle of the twelfth century. Although his father was forced to conform to the religious practices of the Mohammedans, Joseph was taught Hebrew and trained in the study of Hebrew literature. He left his native country about 1185, and went to Egypt, where he continued his scientific pursuits under the tuition of Maimonides, who instructed him in mathematics, astronomy, philosophy and theology. Afterwards (1187) he resided at Aleppo [comp. n. 60 below], and married Sarah, the daughter of Abu'l Ala. After a successful journey to India, he devoted himself chiefly to science, and delivered lectures on various subjects to numerous audiences. He practised as physician to the Emir Faris ad-din Maimun-al-Karsi, and to the King Ed-Dhahir Ghazi, son of Saladin. The Vizir Djemal al-din el-Kofti was his intimate friend. When Charizi came to Aleppo, he found Joseph in the zenith of his career. His poetical talents are praised by Charizi in the eighteenth chapter of the *Tachkemoni*, and in the fiftieth chapter his unparalleled generosity is mentioned. Of his poetical productions, one is named by Charizi (ch. xviii.), and others are referred to by Maimonides in the *Guide*. A Bodleian MS. (Uri, 341) contains a work on the Medicine of the Soul [according to Steinschneider by the same Aknin]. . . . Besides this, Aknin wrote a commentary on the Song of Songs,
34.* and a treatise on the measures mentioned in the Talmud.

60. For the evidence that these incidents occurred in *Bagdad* see Yellin's Hebrew *Maimonides* (1898), p. 67,

Notes

n. 1. The reader is referred to that work for other discussions not included in the present biography.

61. Munk, *Notice*, &c. ; Azariah de Rossi, *Meor Enayim*, end of ch. xxv. ; Yellin, *op. cit.*, p. 72, n. 1.

62. *The Crusades* ("Story of the Nations" Series), p. 305.

63. Lane-Poole, *History of Egypt*, p. 208.

64. *Ibid.*, p. 211.

65. Lane-Poole, *Saladin*, p. 328, from Baha-ed-din, 275.

66. *History of Egypt*, p. 212.

67. This statement is derived from Alkifti ; the very probable identification of Richard I. with the " King of the Franks at Ascalon " is due to Graetz.   35.*

68. On the medical works of Maimonides see Steinschneider, *Heb. Uebersetz.*, § 481 *seq. ;* Hebrew Graetz, iv. 374-5 (with notes), and Appendix, p. 57 ; Yellin, 36.* Hebrew *Maimonides*, p. 73, text and notes.

69. Munk, *Notice*, p. 29.

70. Charizi, *Tachkemoni*, ch. xxix.

71. For the statement of Alkifti and Dscheli see Munk, *Archives Israélites*, 1881, p. 329 ; compare references in note 9 above.

72. Philo, Josephus, Eusebius (*Prep. Ev.* ix. 3), and Arab authors all repeat this theory. See the references in Buxtorff (end of his edition of the *Cusari*), Munk (*Mélanges*, p. 466), and Jellinek (in *Contros Havichuach*). These facts are collected by Harkavy, Appendix to Hebrew Graetz, iv. p. 57.

73. These sentences are aptly used by Dr. Friedländer as the motto to his translation of the *Guide*. See next note.

74. The quotations from the *Guide* are mostly derived from Dr. Friedländer's English translation (London, 1881-85).   The original Arabic, *Dalalat al 'haïrin*, was published with a French translation by Munk (Paris, 1850-1866), his work being entitled *Le Guide des Égarés*. The Arabic MSS. of the *Guide* are enumerated by Dr. Friedländer, *op. cit.* iii. pp. ix. *seq.* The *Guide* is mostly cited by its Hebrew title, *Moreh Nebuchim*.

75. Spinoza, *Theologico-Political Treatise*, ch. vii., severely criticises this principle of Maimonides. " Harm-

Maimonides

ful, useless, absurd," he terms it, but it is clear that he did not fully realise the inwardness of the theory that he was denouncing.

76. Several passages in this account of the *Guide* are repeated from an article by I. Abrahams in *Mind*, xi. pp. 97 *seq.* The reader is referred to the same article for some further discussions of Maimonides' logical method.

77. For an interesting illustration of this see Hirschfeld, *Mohammedan Criticism of the Bible* (*Jewish Quarterly Review*, xiii. pp. 222 *seq.*).

78. On the philosophical import of Maimonides' theory of the divine attributes see Kaufmann, *Geschichte der Attributenlehre in der jüdischen Religionsphilosophie 38.* des Mittelalters*, 1877, pp. 428 *seq.*

79. Friedländer, Analysis, *Guide*, vol. i. p. lxv.

80. Nachmanides opposed this view strongly. See 40.* Friedländer, *ad loc.*

81. Lane-Poole, *History of Egypt*, ch. viii.

82. *Ibid.*, p. 241.

83. *Commentary on Sanhedrin*, x. 1 ; *Aboth*, i. (end). Maimonides had no great affection even for liturgical poems (Geiger, *Melo Chafnaim*, p. 79). Compare 41.* Hebrew Graetz, iv. 330, Appendix, 52.

84. For the evidence of this see Yellin, Hebrew *Maimonides*, p. 97, n. 1.

85. Munk, *Notice*, p. 23. The Essay on the Resurrection was translated into Hebrew by Samuel ibn Tibbon, and also by Charizi. See Steinschneider, *Hebr.* 42.* *Uebersetz.*, 431.

86. An English translation of the Letter by Dr. H. Adler may be found in *Miscellany of Hebrew Literature*, vol. i. (1872). The extract given below is cited from this rendering.

87. Saadiah ibn Danon in *Chemdah Genuza*, p. 30 ; Jedaiah Bedaressi, end of *Bechinath Olam ; Yochasin*, ed. Cracow, p. 131 ; Hebrew Graetz, iv. p. 418. The poems in honour of Maimonides are collected by Steinschneider in his *Kobetz-al-Yad* for the Society Mekitse 44.* Nirdamim.

88. Kaufmann, essay cited in note 92 below, p. 336.

Notes

89. Bacher, *Die Bibelexegese Moses Maimuni's*, 1897; *cf.* also Goldberger, *Die Allegorie in ihrer exegetischen Anwendung bei Moses Maimonides*, 1902.   45.*

90. Guttmann, *Die Scholastik des dreizehnten Jahrhunderts*, 1902, p. 10.   46.*

91. All extant copies of the Arabic original are certainly in Hebrew characters, but Ibn Tibbon used a copy in Arabic characters. (See Friedländer, *Guide*, i. p. xxx, n. 2.)

92. See Steinschneider, *Hebr. Uebersetz.*, p. 432. On the translations in general see Friedländer, *Guide*, vol. iii. pp. xi. *seq.*, and Kaufmann, *Der Fuhrer Maimuni's in der Weltlitteratur* (*Archiv für Geschichte der Philosophie*, xi. pp. 335 *seq.*). Dr. Friedländer also gives a long list of commentaries and works on the *Guide*.   47.*

93. M. Joel, *Verhältniss Albert des Grossen zu Moses Maimonides*, 1863; Guttmann, *Die Scholastik*, p. 85.   50.*

94. Guttmann, *Das Verhältniss des Thomas von Aguind zum Judenthum*, 1891, pp. 31 *seq.*   51.*

95. Saisset, *Maimonide et Spinoza*, in *Revue des Deux Mondes*, 1862.   52.*

96. Guttmann in Brann-Kaufmann's *Monatsschrift*, vol. xxxix., 207; *Die Scholastik*, p. 121.   53.*

97. Guttmann, *ibid.*, vol. xxxviii., 37; *Die Scholastik*, p. 154.   54.*

98. These facts may be found in the later volumes of Graetz.   56.*

99. Solomon Maimon's *Lebensgeschichte*, ii. p. 3; J. C. Murray, *Solomon Maimon: an Autobiography*, 1888, p. xiv. n.   57.*

100. Karl Pearson, *Maimonides and Spinoza*, in *Mind*, vol. viii. pp. 339 *seq.* Pearson finds the parallel to many of Spinoza's characteristic doctrines in the works of Maimonides, especially in the *Code*. "I wished," he says, "to show that the study of Maimonides was traceable even in Spinoza's most finished exposition of his philosophy" (p. 352). So, too, M. Joel (*Zur Genesis der Lehre Spinoza's* 1871) says, p. 6: "Not merely in his youth, but in his maturity, Spinoza was affected by Jewish thought, and among its exponents by Maimonides."   58.*

GENEALOGICAL TABLE

On the basis of a critical study of Joseph Sambary's Chronicle (see note 8, above), Dr. M. Brann has drawn up the following Table (*Monatsschrift*, vol. xliv., 1900, p. 24) :—

MOSES MAIMONIDES
(30, iii. 1135–13, xii. 1204).

ABRAHAM
(17, vi. 1186 to 7, xii. 1237).

OBADIAH
(16, iii. or 5, iv. 1228 to 30, i. 1265).

DAVID
(19, xii. 1212 to 17, viii. 1300).

JACOB
(born 1, ii. 1277).

ISAAC
(12, viii. 1261 born).

SOLOMON
(Nov./Dec. 1248 born).

JOSHUA
(19, viii. 1310–viii./ix. (?) 1355).

ABRAHAM
(7, ix. 1246 to after 1310).

OBADIAH
(born 23, vi. 1297).

MOSES
(born 28, xi. 1290).

Supplementary Notes

By

JACOB I. DIENSTAG

1.* The latest pedigree and geneological table of the Maimonides family was published by Alfred Frei-mann, *Alumah,* vol. I (1936), p. 9-31; 157-158

On the name "Maimon," see M. Steinschneider, *Jewish Quarterly Review,* vol. xi (1899), p. 138; S. Ben Shabbath, *Maimonides Anniversary Volume* (ed. J. L. Fishman), part ii, Jerusalem, 1935, p. 303-308 (Hebrew).

2.* A most remarkable study on "Maimonides in Legend" was written by Isaiah Berger, *Massad,* vol. 2 (1936), p. 216-238 (Hebrew) in which he surveyed the entire subject and included many bibliographical references. The Hebrew *Journal of the Folklore Society in Israel, Yeda-'Am,* upon the occasion of the 750th anniversary of the death of Maimonides, dedicated a major section of its October 1954 issue to the same subject, p. 191-204; 219.

3 * See note 43*.

4.* Only scattered fragments were found of his comments to the Babylonian Talmud, the most complete of which were assembled and edited by M. J. Sachs, Jerusalem, 1963. His work on the Jerusalem Talmud, which also came to us in fragmentary form, was edited by Saul Lieberman: *Hilkhoth ha-Yerushalmi* (The Laws of the Palestinian Talmud) of Rabbi Moses ben Maimon. With introduction, commentary and notes. New York: Jewish Theological Seminary of America, 1947. As to the authenticity of this work,

Supplementary Notes

see review by B. Benedikt, *Kirjath Sepher*, vol. 27
(1951), p. 329-349 (Hebrew).

5.* The anonymous Hebrew translation of this work
was published in: Eliesar Aschkenasi's "Dibré Haka-
mim," Metz, 1849; A. Lichtenberg's edition of "Ko-
bez Teshubot ha-RaMBaM," part 2, Leipzig, 1859,
p. 17-20; J. L. Maimon's Biography of Maimonides,
Jerusalem, 1960, p. 197-211; *Poal ha-Shem* (Collection of works on astronomy), vol. 2, Bné Brak, 1969
(offset of Leipzig, 1859 ed.). An annotated edition
by Lasar Dunner, Frankfort a.M. 1911 who has previously issued a German translation of this work:
Die aelteste astronomische Schrift des Maimonides.
Wurzburg, 1902. It is interesting to note that Chaim
Zelig Slominsky questioned the authenticity of this
work, H*a-Zefirah,* vol. 7, no. 50 (1880), p. 398-399
(Hebrew).

6.* For a list of editions, studies and translations of
Maimonides' *Treatise on Logic,* see, Jacob I. Dienstag, *Aresheth,* vol. 2 (1960). p. 7-34.

7.* On Moses Mendelssohn's commentary to the
Logic of Maimonides, which was published by Sam-
son Kalir who omitted the author's name from the
title page, see, Jacob I. Dienstag, "The Logic of Maimonides During the Haskalah Period," *Hadoar,* vol.
34, no. 22 (April 1, 1955), p. 420-422 (Hebrew).

8.* On Maimonides' attitude towards Islam, see,
A. S. Halkin, Introduction to his edition of the *Epistle to Yemen,* New York: American Academy for
Jewish Research, 1952, p. x-xi; xiii-xxi (Hebrew);
Salo W. Baron, "The Historical Outlook of Maimonides," *Proceedings, American Academy for Jewish
Research,* vol. 6 (1935), p. 71-72; 82-93 [—History
and Jewish Historians, Philadelphia: Jewish Publication Society of America, 1964, p. 146-150]; Michael

Supplementary Notes

Guttmann, "Das Judenthum und seine Umwelt," vol. I, Berlin, 1927, p. 155-157, 193, 367; David S. Shapiro, "Maimonides and the proselyte," *Orthodox Jewish Life,* vol. 23, no. 2 (Dec. 1955), p. 42-44 (contains a digest of responsum of Maimonides to Obadiah the Proselyte concerning proselytes and Islam); L. M. Simmons, "Maimonides and Islam," *Jewish Chronicle,* no. 983 (Jan. 27, 1888), p. 15-16; no. 985 (Feb. 10, 1888), p. 15-16; M. Steinschneider, "Polemische und apologetische Literatur in arabischer Sprache," Leipzig, 1877, p. 353-356.

9.* Some of the literature on the alleged apostasy of Maimonides may be added here: A. Berliner, "Zur Ehrenrettung des Maimonides," Moses ben Maimon (ed. M. Brann, W. Bacher, D. Simonsen & J. Guttmann), vol. 2, Leipzig, 1914, p. 104-130; S. Halberstam, *Jeshurun* (ed. Kabak), vol. 4 (1864), p. 23-36 [—*Maimonides Anniversary Volume* (ed. J. L. Fishman) part 2, p. 134-145]; W. Jawetz, Toledot Yisrael, vol. 12, p. 230-240; J. L. Maimon: *Rabbi Mosheh ben Maimon,* Jerusalem, 1960, p. 242-250; S. L. Rapoport, Kerem Hemed, vol. 6 (1841), p. 114; idem, *Jeshurun* (ed. Kabak), vol. 3 (1857), p. 9-59; N. Slouchz, *Azkarah L'Zecher Harav Kook,* part 4, Jerusalem, 1937, p. 100-127; E. Zweifel, *Hamaggid,* vol. 5 (1861), p. 221-222; 229-237 [—*Maimonides Anniversary Volume* (ed. Fishman), p. 125-134; W. Jawitz, vol. 12, p. 22-229; J. L. Maimon: *Rabbi Mosheh Ben Maimon,* p. 235-242].

10.* A modern Hebrew translation of Maimon's Letter of Consolation was issued by B. Klar and annotated by J. L. Fishman [Maimon], Jerusalem: Mosad Harav Kook, 1945. An abridged version of L. M. Simmon's English translation (*Jewish Quarterly Review,* vol. 2, 1890, p. 62-101) was included in Franz Kobler's "A Treasury of Jewish Letters,"

175

Supplementary Notes

vol. I, Philadelphia: Jewish Publication Society of America, 1953, p. 167-177.

11.* A vocalized Hebrew edition accompanied by a running commentary and introduction, edited by Mordecai Dob Rabinowitz in his collection of *Epistles of Maimonides,* appeared as volume 20 of the *RaMBaM L'Am Series,* Jerusalem: Mosad Harav Kook, 1960. An appraisal of this Epistle and a comparison with Maimonides' *Epistle to Yemen* was written by J. D. Abramsky, *Perakim* (New York), vol. 2 (1960), p. 242-251.

12.* A modern Hebrew translation of this responsum by the late Israel Friedlander was included in Alfred Freimann's edition of the *Responsa of Maimonides,* no. 97, pp. 91-94 [—Blau ed., no. 242, pp. 434-444]. On the Jews of Egypt during the time of Maimonides, referred to in this Responsum, see, Jacob I. Dienstag, "Professor Simha Assaf as a Maimonidean Scholar," *Sinai,* vol. 56 (1964), p. 101-105.

13.* An English extract of Maimonides' letter to Japhet is included in Kobler's "Treasury of Jewish Letters," vol. I, p. 192-193.

14.* A letter by David to Maimonides, written on his way to India from which he never returned, was published by S. D. Goitein, *Ha-Aretz,* vol. 37, Dec. 3, 1954.

15.* A most up to date bibliography of these Arabic texts which were mostly edited by university students as doctoral dissertations, was compiled by A. Yaari, *Kirjath Sepher,* vol. 9 (1932), p. 101-109; 228-235; additions by B. Simches, vol. 12 (1936), p. 132; supplement by Yaari, vol. 29 (1954), p. 176. A new Hebrew translation published simultaneously with

Supplementary Notes

Arabic text and without it was published by Joseph Kapah, Jerusalem: Mosad Harav Kook, 1963-1968.

16.* A critical Hebrew edition with an English translation, introduction and notes was edited by Joseph I. Gorfinkle, New York: Columbia University Press, 1912; vocalized Hebrew edition and commentary by Mordecai Dob Rabinowitz was published in volume 18 of the *RaMBaM L'Am Series,* Jerusalem: Mosad Harav Kook, 1961.

17.* 'To have followed Aristotle here,' Lazarus writes (*The Ethics of Judaism,* Philadelphia: The Jewish Publication Society of America, 1900, vol. I, p. 274), 'was not a happy idea. His ethics, admirable as it is in other respects is especially deficient in logical derivation of its contents ... Yet it is astonishing that Maimonides should have failed to note the infinite divergence between the Aristotelian and the Jewish moral doctrine so completely as to intermingle the two.' Lazarus continues (pp. 275-276), 'What, we ask, has the cycle of Aristotelian virtues gracefully disporting themselves upon the path of the golden-mean-virtues regulating the decorous behavior of the educated, well-to-do Athenian; virtues utterly removed from the serious moral obligation which is of the essence of the Jewish spirit; virtues the lack of which indicates naught of abysmal guilt, the possession of which, naught of the heavenly heights of moral purity before God—what have these comely, amiable virtues to do with the unutterable idea of divine morality?'

It was, however, the neo-Kantian, Hermann Cohen, who came to the rescue of Maimonides in drawing him away from the Aristotelian towards the Platonic 'sphere of influence.' Cohen, in contradistinction to all historians of philosophy, denies Maimonides' close association with the philosophy of Aristotle, espe-

177

Supplementary Notes

cially with his system of ethics. For, according to Aristotle, virtue is only the attainment of bliss. To Maimonides it is the foundation of self-perfection and improvement which leads to Godliness (Hermann Cohen, "Charakteristik der Ethik Maimunis," *Moses ben Maimon,* vol. I, Leipzig, 1908, p. 103ff [—Judische Schriften, vol. 3, Berlin, 1924]. For a full discussion of this subject, see Gorfinkle's edition (see note 16a), pp. 55-62 and Simon Rawidowicz's edition of Maimonides' *Sepher ha-Maddah,* Berlin, 1922, pp. 94-95.

Leon Roth, however, departs from a different premise than do both the critics of Maimonides and his defenders. According to him, Maimonides was not superimposing a Greek ideal on Jewish ethics. "He was taking the formula upon which Aristotle brought the practice of the Greek ideal, and with its help brought into order the material afforded him by Jewish tradition' (Leon Roth: The Guide for the Perplexed: Moses Maimonides, London: Hutchinson's Library, [1950], p. 105). Roth here reiterates his views expressed some years ago in an essay entitled "Supremacy of Reason," *Moznaim,* vol. 3 (1935) p. 378 ff. (Hebrew). See, also, on the general aspect of this subject, Harry S. Lewis, The "Golden Mean" in Judaism, *Jewish Studies in Memory of Israel Abrahams,* New York, 1927, p. 283-295.

18.* English translation of Maimonides *Articles of Faith* by J. Abelson, "Maimonides on the Jewish Creed," *Jewish Quarterly Review,* vol. 19 (1907), pp. 24-58; Arnold Jacob Wolf, *Judaism,* vol. 15 (1966), pp. 95-101; 211-216; 337-342.

19.* Besides the hymn *Yigdal,* there are close to 100 poems on this theme. See, Alexander Marx, "A List of Poems on the Articles of the Creed," *Jewish Quarterly Review,* N.S., vol. 9 (1919), p. 305-336; Israel

Supplementary Notes

Davidson, "Thesaurus of Mediaeval Hebrew Poetry," vol. 4, p. 493 in which he indexed the poems on the *Thirteen Articles of Faith* enumerated in his work.

20.* Crescas' and Albo's criticism of Maimonides' Articles of Faith is discussed by Meyer Waxman, "Maimonides as Dogmatist," *Central Conference of American Rabbis, Yearbook,* vol. 45 (1935), p. 397-418.

21.* English translation by Boaz Cohen in A. S. Halkin's critical edition of the *Epistle to Yemen*. The Arabic Original and the Three Hebrew Versions, edited from manuscripts with introduction and notes. New York: American Academy for Jewish Research, 1952. For a bibliography of editions, translations and studies on the subject, see Jacob I. Dienstag, *Aresheth,* vol. 3 (1961), pp. 48-70.

22.* This view is not shared by Halkin. See introduction to the *Epistle,* p. xi.

23.* Nachmanides' *Letter to the French Rabbis* was also edited by C. Chavel with introduction and notes in his "Kitvé Rabenu Mosheh ben Nahman," vol. I, Jerusalem: Mosad Harav Kook, 1963, pp. 333-351; the above mentioned reference to the *Kaddish* in which the grateful Yemenite Jews included the name of Maimonides is on p. 341.

24.* Alfred Freimann succeeded to assemble the most complete collection of Responsa of Maimonides, edited with scolarly annotations, introduction and analytic index. It contains 386 responsa. Jerusalem: Mekize Nirdamim, 1934. He was followed by J. Blau who utilized Freimann's edition and notes and issued the *Responsa* with the Arabic original (where available). It contains 459 responsa. 3 volumes. Jerusalem: Mekize Nirdamim, 1957-1961.

Supplementary Notes

25.* This letter to Joseph Ibn Gabir appeared in abridged English translation in Kobler's "Treasury of Jewish Letters," vol. I, p. 198-201.

26.* This letter to Obadiah the Proselyte, appeared in an abridged English translation in Kobler, loc. cit. p. 194-196.

27.* As to the date of the publication of the *Mishneh Torah,* Solomon Gandz, "Date of the completion of Maimonides' Code," *Proceedings of the American Academy for Jewish Research,* vol. 17 (1947-48), p. 1-7.

28.* Cf. Jacob I. Dienstag, *En Ha-Mizwot;* Bio-Bibliographical Lexicon of the Scholarship Pertaining to the *Sefer Ha-Mizwot* of Moses Maimonides. New York: Talpioth, Yeshiva University, 1968; also: *Sefer Ha-Mizwot;* Bibliography of Editions, Translations and Studies. It is to appear in the forthcoming issue of *Aresheth,* volume 5.

29.* See also, Isadore Twersky, Rabad of Posquières. Cambridge: Harvard University Press, 1962.

30.* The passage on the founders of Christianity and Islam in *Mishneh Torah, Hilkot Melakim,* XI:4 was deleted from most editions of the *Code* due to censorship. It was reintroduced in the *RaMBaM L'Am* edition. Jerusalem: Mosad Harav Kook, vol. 14, 1962, pp. 415-417. English translation by Abraham M. Hershman: The Code of Maimonides, Book XIV: The Book of Judges. New Haven: Yale University Press, 1949, p. xxiii-xxiv.

31.* On Maimonides as codifier, see: Irving M. Levey, *Yearbook Central Conference of American Rabbis,* vol. 45 (1935), p. 368-396; Isidore Epstein, *Moses Maimonides* 1135-1204; *Anglo-Jewish Papers*

Supplementary Notes

in Connection with the Eighth Centenary of his birth.
London: Soncino, [1935], p. 59-82; Isaac Herzog, ibid, p. 135-153; A. Marmorstein, ibid, p. 155-174; Chaim Tchernowitz, "Maimonides as Codifier," New York: Maimonides Octocentennial Committee, 1935, Jacob I. Dienstag, [new] *Encyclopedia Judaica* (c. 1971), vol. XI, col. 764-768.

32.* The latest bibliography of commentaries to the *Mishneh Torah* was compiled by Judah Rubinstein. *Mishneh Torah,* New York; Schulsinger Bros., 1947, vol. 5. For the latest bibliography of *Mishneh Torah* editions (1480-1970), see, Jacob I. Dienstag, *Studies in Jewish Bibliography, History and Literature in Honor of I. Edward Kiev,* New York: Ktav, 1971, p. 21-108 (Hebrew section).

33.* On Samuel ben Ali and his relation to Maimonides, see Simha Assaf, *Tarbiz,* vol. I, (1931); Introduction by Mordecai Dob Rabinowitz to *Letters of Maimonides* (RaMBaM L'Am edition), Jerusalem: Mosad Harav Kook, 1969, p. 257-264; Jacob Mann, Texts and Studies, vol. I, Cincinnati, 1931, p. 214ff; 251-253; Jacob I. Dienstag, *Sinai,* vol. 56 (1965), p. 113-115 in which bibliographical material relating to the above study by Assaf is listed.

34.* Concerning the question whether there were two people by the same name, Joseph b. Jehudah; one for whom the *Guide for the Perplexed* was written and another—only a friend of Maimonides (which is the opinion of Munk) or as Steinschneider believed that there was only one person, see the literature listed in Jacob I. Dienstag, "Moritz Steinschneider as a Maimonidean Scholar," Sinai, vol. 66 (1970), p. 363-364. Joseph Ibn Aknin's *Commentary to the Song of Songs,* was edited by A. S. Halkin, Jerusalem: Mekize Nirdamim, 1964. D. H. Baneth

Supplementary Notes

has edited the correspondence between Maimonides and his disciple on the basis of manuscripts with introductions and explanatory notes. Jerusalem: Mekize Nirdamim, 1946.

35.* Bernard Lewis refutes the theory that Maimonides was the court-physician of Saladin and that he was invited by Richard Lionheart to treat him. "Maimonides, Lionheart, and Saladin," *Eretz-Israel,* vol. 7 (1964), pp. 70-75.

36.* For an up to date list of the medical works of Maimonides, and the literature thereon, see, Fred Rosner, "Maimonides the Physician: a bibliography," *Bulletin of the History of Medicine,* vol. 43 (1969), p. 221-235.

37.* Modern scholars differ whether Maimonides was the *Nagid* (official head of the Jewish community) in Egypt. See the literature in Jacob I. Dienstag's study in *Sinai,* vol. 56 (1964), p. 103.

38.* For the literature on Maimonides' theory of divine attributes, see, Jacob I. Dienstag, *Studies in Bibliography and Booklore,* vol. 5 (1961), pp. 23-27 (Hebrew section).

39.* For the literature on Maimonides' theory of prophecy, see, Jacob I. Dienstag, "Wilhelm Bacher as a Maimonidean Scholar," *Sinai,* vol. 55 (1964), p. 68-69; idem, "Biblical Exegesis of Maimonides in Jewish Scholarship," *Samuel K. Mirsky Memorial Volume,* New York: Yeshiva University, [1970], p. 163; 174-179.

40.* On Nachmanides' criticism of Maimonides and those who rose to defend him, see, Jacob I. Dienstag, "Biblical Exegesis of Maimonides in Jewish Scholarship," loc. cit. p. 183-187.

Supplementary Notes

41.* Maimonides, nevertheless, did compose some poems, some of which were included in the *Neilah* Services of Yom Kippur. See the literature on this subject and his attitude towards music, Jacob I. Dienstag, "Wilhelm Bacher as a Maimonidean Scholar," loc. cit. p. 80-82.

42.* The Essay appeared in a critical edition: Maimonides' Treatise on Resurrection...The original Arabic and Samuel Ibn Tibbon's Hebrew translation and glossary. Edited with critical apparatus, notes and introduction by Joshua Finkel. New York: American Academy for Jewish Research, 1939. English translation from the Hebrew version by Sabato Morais appeared in the *Jewish Messenger,* 1859, p. 82-83; 90-91; 98; 106; 114.

43.* A critical edition of his *Letter to the Rabbis of Marseilles,* was published by Alexander Marx, "The Correspondence between the Rabbis of Southern France and Maimonides on Astrology," *Hebrew Union College Annual,* vol. 3 (1926), p. 311-358; "Additions and corrections," ibid, vol. 4 (1927), p. 493-494. English translation by Ralph Lerner, in "Medieval Political Philosophy" (ed. R. Lerner and M. Mahdi). New York: Free Press of Glencoe, (c. 1963), p. 227-236; Analysis of the Letter by R. Lerner, "Maimonides' Letter on Astrology," *History of Religions,* 8 (1968), p. 143-158.

44.* The poems in honour of Maimonides, edited by M. Steinschneider (referred to by the authors in note 87) were published in *Kobetz-al-Yad,* vol. 1 (1885), p. 1-32; vol. 2 (1886), p. 33-37. Some of these poems were re-edited with vowel points and notes by H. Brody, *Moznaim,* vol. 3 (1935), p. 402-413. See on this subject J. I. Dienstag, "Moritz Steinschneider as a Maimonidean Scholar," *Sinai,* vol. 66 (1970), p. 350-352.

Supplementary Notes

45.* Bacher's work was translated into Hebrew, Tel-Aviv, 1932. Analysis of this work by Jacob I. Dienstag, "Wilhelm Bacher as a Maimonidean Scholar," loc. cit. p. 65-72.

46.* Guttmann has continued his studies on this theme in his "Der Einfluss der maimonidischen Philosophie auf das christliche Abenland," *Moses ben Maimon* (ed. Bacher, Brann & Simonsen), vol. 1, Leipzig, 1908, p. 135-230.

47.* Kaufmann's study was reprinted in his "Gesammelte Schriften," vol. 2, Frankfurt a.M. 1910, p. 152-189 and was translated into Hebrew, "Mehkarim...", Jerusalem: Mosad Harav Kook, 1962, p. 214-238. The most complete bibliography of commentaries to the *Guide for the Perplexed* was compiled by M. Steinschneider, "Hebräischen Commentare zum Fuhrer des Maimonides," *Festschrift zum siebzigsten Geburtstage A. Berliner's,* Frankfurt a.M., 1903, p. 345-363.

48.* On Alexander Hales' indebtedness to Maimonides, see, Jakob Guttmann, "Alexandre de Hales et le Judaism," *Revue des Etudes Juives,* vol. 19 (1889), p. 229-234; Die Scholastik des dreizehnten Jahrhunderts in ihren Beziehungen zum Judenthum und zur judischen Literatur, Breslau, 1902, p. 41-46; *Moses ben Maimon* loc. cit., p. 147-152.

49.* On William of Auvergne, see, J. Guttmann, "Guillaume d'Auvergne et la littérature Juive," *Revue des Etudes Juives, vol.* 18 (1889), p. 247-251; p. 247-251; Die Scholastik, p. 17-26; *Moses ben Maimon,* loc. cit., p. 140-147.

50.* Joel's study on Albertus Magnus was reprinted in his "Beitraege zur Geschichte der Philosophie," Band I, Breslau, 1876, p. 1-48. See also, J. Guttmann,

Supplementary Notes

Moses ben Maimon, loc. cit. p. 153-175; Adalbert Merz, "Die Prophetie des Joel," Halle a.S., 1879, p. 368-375; Anselm Rohner, "Das Schöpfungsproblem bei Moses Maimonides, Albertus Magnus und Thomas von Aquin," Munster, 1913; Pièrre Duhem, "Le Système du Monde," vol. 5, Paris, 1917, p. 443-440.

51.* On Thomas Aquinas, see also: J. Guttmann, *Moses ben Maimon,* loc. cit., p. 175-204; Z. Diesendruck "Address on Maimonides and Thomas Aquinas," [Chicago, 1938]; Harry A. Wolfson, "The Kalam arguments for creation in Saadia, Averroes, Maimonides and St. Thomas," *Saadia Anniversary Volume,* New York: American Academy for Jewish Research, 1943, p. 197-245; Harry Blumberg, "The Problem of Immortality in Avicenna, Maimonides and St. Thomas," *Harry A. Wolfson Jubilee Volume,* vol. I, Jerusalem, 1965, p. 165-185.

52.* Saisset's study appeared also in German, "Die Philosophie der Juden," *Monatsschrift fur Geschichte und Wissenschaft des Judenthums,* vol. XI (1862), p. 445-471. E. Saisset was a Catholic philosopher who translated Spinoza into French.

53.* Pagination for this note to be corrected: *Monatsschrift,* vol. xxxix, p. 216 (not 207); Die Scholastik, p. 131 (not 121). The above material was incorporated in Louis I. Newman's "Jewish Influence on Christian Reform Movements," New York: Columbia University Press, 1925, p. 116-117.

54.* See also, J. Guttmann in *Moses ben Maimon,* loc. cit., p. 206-208.

55.* Not exactly! Long after Descartes (1596-1650), Leibniz (1646-1716), commented upon the *Guide* which were published by Count Louis Alexandre

Supplementary Notes

Foucher de Careil, "Leibniz la Philosophie Juive et la Cabale," Paris, 1861. See, Guttmann, *Moses ben Maimon*, loc. cit., p. 224-230; S. Atlas, "The Philosophy of Maimonides and its systematic place in the history of philosophy," *Philosophy*, vol. XI (Jan. 1936), p. 60-75; N. Ulmann, "Leibniz lecteur de Maimonide," *Les Nouveaux Cahiers*, vol. 24 (Sept. 1971), p. 13-17.

56.* On Maimonides in the Hashkalah period, see F. Lachover, *Moznaim*, vol. 3 (1935), p. 539-546 [—Al Gvul ha-Yashan ve-ha-Hadash, Jerusalem: Mosad Bialik, 1951, p. 97-107]; Joseph Schechter, *Perakim* (Haifa), no. 9 (1958), p. 312 [—Limudei ha-Yahaduth, Tel-Aviv: Yavneh, 1968, p. 107-110]; P. Kon, *Yivo Bletter*, vol. 13 (1938) {—*Wachstein Memorial Volume*}, p. 577-582 Joseph I. Schneersohn, "The Tzemach Tzedek and the Haskalah Movement," Brooklyn, N.Y.: Kehot, 1962; Judah Rosenthal, *Perakim* (New York), vol. 2 (1960), p. 45-53 [—Mehkarim u-Mekoroth, Jerusalem: R. Mass, 1967, p. 117-125]; Jacob I. Dienstag, *Hadoar*, vol. 34, no. 22 (April 1, 1955), p. 420-422.

57.* On Solomon Maimon's relation to the philosophy of Maimonides, see Samuel Atlas, "From Critical to Speculative Idealism; the philosophy of Solomon Maimon," Hague: M. Nijhoff, 1964; Hugo Bergmann, "The Philosophy of Solomon Maimon." Translated from the Hebrew by Noah J. Jacobs, Jerusalem: Magnes Press, 1967, p. 210-215.

58.* Karl Pearson's study was reprinted in his "The Ethic of Freethought and other Addresses and Essays," London: Unwin, 1888, p. 125-142; second edition, revised, London: A. C. Black, 1901, p. 135-155. For further elaboration on this point see, Harry A. Wolfson, "The Philosophy of Spinoza," vol. 2, Cambridge: Harvard University Press, 1934 (see

Supplementary Notes

indexes, p. 387-388; 415-416); idem, "Some guiding principles in determining Spinoza's mediaeval sources," *Jewish Quarterly Review,* N. S. vol. 27 (1937), p. 334-337; Leon Roth, "Spinoza, Descartes and Maimonides," Oxford: Clarendon Press, 1924; Jacob I. Dienstag, "Biblical Exegesis of Maimonides in Jewish Scholarship," *Samuel K. Mirsky Memorial Volume,* New York: Yeshiva University, 1970, p. 180-182.

INDEX

189

Index

Index

Index

his attitude towards Karaism, **43, 79, 81** ; his early life in Cairo, **45** ; death of Maimon, **47** ; Maimonides becomes physician, **48** ; the *Siraj* completed (1168), **49** ; characteristics of the *Siraj*, chap. v. ; the *Eight Chapters*, **56**, note ; the doctrine of the mean, **57** ; resurrection and immortality, **61** ; the Jewish creed, **65** ; the Yemenites, *Letter to the South*, **74** ; his " Responsa," **79** *seq.* ; the *Mishneh Torah* (1180), chap. vii. ; the *Sefer Hamitzvoth*, **88** ; Attacks on the *Mishneh Torah*, **92**, chap. viii., **151** ; eulogies of Maimonides' work, chap. viii. ; controversy with Samuel ben Ali of Bagdad, **101** ; friendship with Joseph Aknin, **103, 120** ; birth of his son Ahaham, **108**; the second crusade, chap. ix. ; Maimonides and Richard Cœur de Lion, **113** ; physician to Alfadhel, ibid.; Abdel-Latif's judgment on Maimonides, **115** ; charge of relapse from Islam, **117** ; *Guide of the Perplexed* (1190), chap. x. ; Maimonides and Aristotle, **125** ; allegories in Scripture, **128** ; on the Divine Attributes, **130** ; on prophecy,

131 ; on the meaning of the Pentateuch, **134**; on sacrifices, **135**; last years of Maimonides (193–1204), chap. xi. ; Maimonides on poetry, **141** ; *Epistle on the Resurrection*, **142** ; on astrology, **144** ; letter to Samuel ibn Tibbon, **148** ; death of Maimonides, **150**; his influence on Jewish and general thought, chap. xii.; genealogy of the family of Maimonides (end of " Notes ")

Maimonists and anti-Maimonists, **151, 152**

Martel, Charles, **5**

Medical works of Maimonides, **114, 115**

Medresa, the, **86, 87**

Mendelssohn, Moses, **21, 158**

Mesopotamia, **85, 87**

Messiahs, false, **73–75, 77**

Metaphysics, Maimonides on, **119, 120** (*Guide of the Perplexed*)

Mishnah, **7** ; exposition of before the time of Maimonides, **22** ; commentary of Obadiah of Bertinoro, **52** ; Maimonides' commentary on, **21–23, 49, 52–57, 61–68, 155**. For editions of Arabic text, see note **23**

Mishneh Torah of Maimonides, **88–96, 151, 153, 154**; defects in, **91, 92** ; *Sefer Hamada*, **94** ; popularity

192

Index

of, **97**, **98**; opposition to, **98–103**; *see also* note 47

Moors, *see* Cordova

Morocco, **17**

Mutakallemim, Arabian, **125–127**

NACHMANIDES, **81**, and notes 37, **80**

Nureddin, **40-42**, **70-72**, **86**

OMEYYADES, **1–4**

PALESTINE, **38**, **70**, **71**, **85**, **110**, **111**, **150**

Pleasures of music, &c., Maimonides' attitude towards, **141**, **142**

Professional teachers, Maimonides' denunciation of, **46**

Prophecy, theory of, **132– 134**, **156** (*Guide of the Perplexed*)

Pumbaditha, **6**

RABBINICAL literature, Maimonides' views on, **53**, **54**

" Responsa " of Maimonides, **78–84**, and note 39

Resurrection of the dead, epistle on, **142**, **143**, and note 85

Reward and punishment, Maimonides' views on, **62–65** (*Commentary on the Mishnah*)

Richard Cœur-de-Lion, **71**, **110**, **111**, **113**

Roderick, **5**

SACRIFICES, theory of, **135**, **136** (*Guide of the Perplexed*)

Saladin, **40-42**, **50**, **70-73**, **78**, **85–87**, **110-112**, **115**, **116**, **139**

Sambary, quoted, note 8 and **172**

Samuel ben Ali of Bagdad, **101**, **104–107**, **117**, **142**, and note 57

Samuel the Nagid, **7**, **18**

Samuel ibn Tibbon, **145– 148**, **156**

Sanhedrin, treatise (*Commentary on the Mishnah*), **56**

Shawar, **41**, **49**

Shirkuh, **40**, **41**, **49**

Shulchan Aruch, **91**, **154**

Siraj, *see* Mishnah, commentary on

Sora, **6**

South, Maimonides' letter to the, **74–78**, and notes **13**, **35**, **36**

Spain, **152**; Jewish love for, **3**

Spanish influences on Judaism, **6**, **7**

Spinoza, **122**, **159**, **160**, and notes **75**, **95**, **100**

Sudanese, **70**, **71**

Syria, **85–87**, **146**

TALMUD, Maimonides on students of, **55**; effect of Maimonides' work in the study of, **90**, **91**, **93**

Tarik, **5**

Teman, *see* South

M

Index